# The Seven
# Good Years

ALSO BY ETGAR KERET

*Suddenly, a Knock on the Door*

*The Girl on the Fridge*

*Missing Kissinger*

*The Nimrod Flipout*

*The Bus Driver Who Wanted to Be God
& Other Stories*

# The Seven Good Years

## A MEMOIR

### ETGAR KERET

Translated by Sondra Silverston,
Miriam Shlesinger,
Jessica Cohen, Anthony Berris

GRANTA

Granta Publications, 12 Addison Avenue, London W11 4QR

First published in Great Britain by Granta Books, 2015
First published in the United States by Riverhead Books,
an imprint of Penguin Random House LLC, New York, 2015

This book has been selected to receive financial assistance from English PEN's
Writers in Translation programme supported by Bloomberg. English PEN exists
to promote literature and its understanding, uphold writers' freedoms around
the world, campaign against the persecution and imprisonment of writers for
stating their views, and promote the friendly co-operation of writers and free
exchange of ideas. www.englishpen.org

A CIP catalogue record for this book is available from the British Library.

1 3 5 7 9 10 8 6 4 2

ISBN 978 1 78378 046 4 (hardback)
ISBN 978 1 78378 048 8 (ebook)

Book design by Amanda Dewey
Illustrations © by Jason Polan

Offset by Avon DataSet Ltd, Bidford on Avon, Warwickshire

Printed and bound by CPI Group (UK) Ltd, Croydon, CR0 4YY

www.grantabooks.com

*To my mother*

# Contents

**YEAR ONE**

Suddenly, the Same Thing   *3*

Big Baby   *7*

Call and Response   *11*

The Way We War   *15*

**YEAR TWO**

Yours, Insincerely   *21*

Flight Meditation   *24*

Strange Bedfellows   *28*

Defender of the People   *33*

Requiem for a Dream   *37*

Long View   *43*

**YEAR THREE**

Throwdown at the Playground   *51*

Swede Dreams   *56*

Matchstick War   60

Idol Worship   64


## YEAR FOUR

Bombs Away   71

What Does the Man Say?   76

My Lamented Sister   80

Bird's Eye   86


## YEAR FIVE

Imaginary Homeland   93

Fat Cats   96

Poser   101

Just Another Sinner   105

Shit Happens   108

Last Man Standing   111

Bemusement Park   115


## YEAR SIX

Ground Up   123

Sleepover   129

Boys Don't Cry   133

Accident   135

A Mustache for My Son   140

Love at First Whiskey   144

## YEAR SEVEN

Shiva  *151*

In My Father's Footsteps  *155*

Jam  *159*

Fare and Good  *164*

Pastrami  *169*

# The Seven
# Good Years

# Year One

# Suddenly, the Same Thing

I just hate terrorist attacks," the thin nurse says to the older one. "Want some gum?"

The older nurse takes a piece and nods. "What can you do?" she says. "I also hate emergencies."

"It's not the emergencies," the thin one insists. "I have no problem with accidents and things. It's the terrorist attacks, I'm telling you. They put a damper on everything."

Sitting on the bench outside the maternity ward, I think to myself, She's got a point. I got here just an hour ago, all excited, with my wife and a neat-freak taxi driver who, when my wife's water broke, was afraid it would ruin his upholstery. And now I'm sitting in the hallway, feeling glum, waiting for the staff to come back from the ER. Everyone but the two nurses has gone to help treat the people injured in the attack. My wife's contractions have slowed down, too. Probably even the baby feels this whole getting-born thing isn't that urgent anymore. As I'm on my way to the cafeteria, a few of the injured roll past on squeaking gurneys. In the taxi on the way to the hospital, my wife was screaming like a madwoman, but all these people are quiet.

"Are you Etgar Keret?" a guy wearing a checked shirt asks me. "The writer?" I nod reluctantly. "Well, what do you know?" he says, pulling a tiny tape recorder out of his bag. "Where were you when it happened?" he asks. When I hesitate for a second, he says in a show of empathy: "Take your time. Don't feel pressured. You've been through a trauma."

"I wasn't in the attack," I explain. "I just happen to be here today. My wife's giving birth."

"Oh," he says, not trying to hide his disappointment, and presses the stop button on his tape recorder. *"Mazal tov."* Now he sits down next to me and lights himself a cigarette.

"Maybe you should try talking to someone else," I suggest as an attempt to get the Lucky Strike smoke out of my face. "A minute ago, I saw them take two people into neurology."

"Russians," he says with a sigh, "don't know a word of Hebrew. Besides, they don't let you into neurology anyway. This is my seventh attack in this hospital, and I know all their shtick by now." We sit there a minute without talking. He's about ten years younger than I am but starting to go bald. When he catches me looking at him, he smiles and says, "Too bad you weren't there. A reaction from a writer would've been good for my article. Someone original, someone with a little vision. After every attack, I always get the same reactions: 'Suddenly I heard a boom,' 'I don't know what happened,' 'Everything was covered in blood.' How much of that can you take?"

"It's not their fault," I say. "It's just that the attacks are always the same. What kind of original thing can you say about an explosion and senseless death?"

"Beats me," he says with a shrug. "You're the writer."

Some people in white jackets are starting to come back from the ER on their way to the maternity ward. "You're from Tel Aviv," the reporter says to me, "so why'd you come all the way to this dump to give birth?"

"We wanted a natural birth. Their department here—"

"Natural?" he interrupts, sniggering. "What's natural about a midget with a cable hanging from his belly button popping out of your wife's vagina?" I don't even try to respond. "I told my wife," he continues, "'If you ever give birth, only by Caesarean section, like in America. I don't want some baby stretching you out of shape for me.' Nowadays, it's only in primitive countries like this that women give birth like animals. *Yallah*, I'm going to work." Starting to get up, he tries one more time. "Maybe you have something to say about the attack anyway?" he asks. "Did it change anything for you? Like what you're going to name the baby or something, I don't know." I smile apologetically. "Never mind," he says with a wink. "I hope it goes easy, man."

Six hours later, a midget with a cable hanging from his belly button comes popping out of my wife's vagina and immediately starts to cry. I try to calm him down, to convince him that there's nothing to worry about. That by the time he grows up, everything here in the Middle East will be settled: peace will come, there won't be any more terrorist attacks, and even if once in a blue moon there is one, there will always be someone original, someone with a little vision, around to describe it perfectly. He quiets down and then considers his next move. He's supposed to be naive—seeing as how he's a newborn—but even he doesn't buy it, and after a second's hesitation and a small hiccup, he goes back to crying.

# Big Baby

When I was a kid, my parents took me to Europe. The high point of the trip wasn't Big Ben or the Eiffel Tower but the flight from Israel to London—specifically, the meal. There on the tray were a tiny can of Coca-Cola and, next to it, a box of cornflakes not much bigger than a pack of cigarettes.

My surprise at the miniature packages didn't turn into genuine excitement until I opened them and discovered that the Coke tasted like the Coke in regular-size cans and the cornflakes were real, too. It's hard to explain where that excitement actually came from. All we're talking about is a soft drink and a breakfast cereal in much smaller packages, but when I was seven, I was sure I was witnessing a miracle.

Today, thirty years later, sitting in my living room in Tel Aviv and looking at my two-week-old son, I have exactly the same feeling: Here's a man who weighs no more than ten pounds—but inside he's angry, bored, frightened, and serene, just like any other man on this planet. Put a three-piece suit and a Rolex on him, stick a tiny attaché case in his hand, and send him out into the world, and he'll negotiate, do battle, and close deals without even blinking. He doesn't talk, that's true. And he soils himself as if there were no tomorrow. I'm the first to admit he has a thing or two to learn before he can be shot into space or allowed to fly an F-16. But in principle, he's a complete person wrapped in a nineteen-inch package, and not just any person, but one who's very extreme, an eccentric, a character. The kind you respect but may not completely understand. Because, like all complex people, regardless of their height or weight, he has many sides.

*My son, the enlightened one:* As someone who has read a lot about Buddhism and has listened to two or three lectures given by gurus and even once had diarrhea in India, I have to say that my baby son is the first enlightened person I have ever met. He truly lives in the present: He never bears a grudge, never fears the future. He's totally ego-free. He never tries to defend his honor or take credit. His grandparents, by the way, have already opened a savings account for him, and every time they rock him in his cradle, Grandpa tells him about the excellent interest rate he managed to get for him and how much money, at an anticipated single-digit average inflation rate, he'll have in twenty-one years, when the account comes due. The little one makes no reply. But then Grandpa calculates the percentages against the prime interest rate, and I notice a few wrinkles appearing on my son's forehead—the first cracks in the wall of his nirvana.

*My son, the junkie:* I'd like to apologize to all the addicts and reformed addicts reading this, but with all due respect to them and their suffering, nobody's jones can touch my son's. Like every true addict, he doesn't have the same options others do when it comes to spending leisure time—those familiar choices of a good book, an evening stroll, or the NBA play-offs. For him, there are only two possibilities: a breast or hell. "Soon you'll discover the world—girls, alcohol, illegal online gambling," I say, trying to soothe him. But until that happens, we both know that only the breast will exist. Lucky for him, and for us, he has a mother equipped with two. In the worst-case scenario, if one breaks down, there's always a spare.

*My son, the psychopath:* Sometimes when I wake up at night and see his little figure shaking next to me in the bed like a toy burning through its batteries, producing strange guttural noises, I can't help comparing him in my imagination to Chucky in the horror movie *Child's Play*. They're the same height, they have the same temperament, and neither holds anything sacred. That's the truly unnerving thing about my two-week-old son: he doesn't have a drop of morality, not an ounce. Racism, inequality, insensitivity, globalization—he couldn't care less. He has no interest in anything beyond his immediate drives and desires. As far as he's concerned, other people can go to hell or join Greenpeace. All he wants now is some fresh milk or relief for his diaper rash, and if the world has to be destroyed for him to get it, just show him the button. He'll press it without a second thought.

*My son, the self-hating Jew . . .*

"Don't you think that's enough?" my wife says, cutting in. "Instead of dreaming up hysterical accusations against your adorable son, maybe you could do something useful and change him?"

"OK," I tell her. "OK, I was just finishing up."

# Call and Response

I really admire considerate telemarketers who listen and try to sense your mood without immediately forcing a dialogue on you when they call. That's why, when Devora from YES, the satellite TV company, calls and asks if it's a good time for me to talk, the first thing I do is thank her for her thoughtfulness. Then I tell her politely that no, it isn't.

"The thing is, just a minute ago I fell into a hole and injured my forehead and foot, so this really isn't the ideal time," I explain.

"I understand," Devora says. "So when do you think it'll be a good time to talk? An hour?"

"I'm not sure," I say. "My ankle must have broken when I fell, and the hole is pretty deep. I don't think I'll be able to climb out without help. So it pretty much depends on how quickly the rescue team gets here and whether they have to put my foot in a cast or not."

"So, maybe I should call tomorrow?" she suggests, unruffled.

"Yes," I groan. "Tomorrow sounds great."

"What's all that business with the hole?" my wife, next to me in a taxi, rebukes after hearing my evasive tactics. This is the first time we have gone out and left our son, Lev, with my mother, so she is a little edgy. "Why can't you just say, 'Thanks, but I'm not interested in buying, renting, or borrowing whatever it is you're selling, so please don't call me again, not in this life, and if possible, not in the next one, either.' Then pause briefly and say, 'Have a nice day.' And hang up, like everyone else."

I don't think everyone else is as firm and nasty to Devora and her ilk as my wife is, but I must admit she has a point. In the Middle East, people feel their mortality more than anywhere else on the planet, which causes most of the population to develop aggressive tendencies toward strangers who try to waste the little time they have left on earth. And though I guard my time just as jealously, I have a real problem saying no to strangers on the phone. I have no trouble shaking off vendors in the outdoor market or saying no to a friend who offers me something on the phone. But the unholy combination of a phone request plus a stranger paralyzes me, and in less than a second, I'm imagining the scarred face of the person on the other end who has led a life of suffering and humiliation. I picture him standing on the window ledge of his forty-second-floor office talking to me on a cordless phone in a calm voice, but he's already made up his mind: "One more asshole hangs up on me and I jump!" And when it comes down to deciding between a person's life and getting hooked up to the "Balloon Sculpture:

Endless Fun for the Whole Family" channel for only 9.99 shekels a month, I choose life, or at least I did until my wife and financial adviser politely asked me to stop.

That's when I began to develop the "poor Grandma strategy," which invokes a woman for whom I've arranged dozens of virtual burials in order to get out of futile conversations. But since I'd already dug myself a hole and fallen into it for Devora of the satellite TV concern, I could actually let Grandma Shoshana rest in peace this time.

"Good morning, Mr. Keret," Devora says the next day. "I hope this is a better time for you."

"The truth is, there were a few complications with my foot," I mumble. "I don't know how, but gangrene developed. And you've caught me right before the amputation."

"It'll just take a minute," she gamely tries.

"I'm sorry," I insist. "They already gave me a sedative and the doctor is signaling for me to close my cell phone. He says it isn't sterilized."

"So I'll try tomorrow, then," Devora says. "Good luck with the amputation."

Most telemarketers give up after one call. Phone pollsters and Internet-surfing-package sellers may call back for another round. But Devora from the satellite TV company is different.

"Hello, Mr. Keret," she says when I answer the next call, unprepared. "How are you?" Before I can reply, she goes on: "Since your new medical condition will probably keep you at home, I thought I'd offer you our Extreme Sports package. Four channels that include various extreme sports from all around the world, from the dwarf-hurling world championship games to the Australian glass-eating matches."

"Do you want Etgar?" I whisper.

"Yes," Devora says.

"He died," I say, and pause before continuing to whisper. "Such a tragedy. An intern finished him off on the operating table. We're thinking about suing."

"So who am I talking to?" Devora asks.

"Michael, his younger brother," I improvise. "But I can't talk now, I'm at the funeral."

"I'm sorry for your loss," Devora says in a shaky voice. "I didn't get to speak with him a lot, but he sounded like a lovely person."

"Thank you," I keep whispering. "I have to hang up. I have to say Kaddish now."

"Of course," Devora says. "I'll call later. I have a consolation deal that's just perfect for you."

# The Way We War

Yesterday I called the cell phone company people to yell at them. The day before, my best friend, Uzi, told me he'd called and yelled at them a little, threatened to switch to another provider. And they immediately lowered their price by fifty shekels a month. "Can you believe it?" my friend said excitedly. "One angry five-minute call and you save six hundred shekels a year."

The customer-service representative was named Tali. She listened silently to all my complaints and threats, and when I finished, she said in a low, deep voice: "Tell me, sir, aren't you ashamed of yourself? We're at war. People are getting killed. Missiles are falling on Haifa and Tiberias, and all you can think about is your fifty shekels?"

There was something to that, something that made me slightly uncomfortable. I apologized immediately, and the noble

Tali quickly forgave me. After all, war is not exactly the right time to bear a grudge against one of your own.

That afternoon I decided to test the effectiveness of the Tali argument on a stubborn taxi driver who refused to take me and my baby son in his cab because I didn't have a car seat with me.

"Tell me, aren't you ashamed of yourself?" I said, trying to quote Tali as precisely as I could. "We're at war. People are getting killed. Missiles are falling on Tiberias, and all you can think about is a damn car seat?"

The argument worked here like magic, and the embarrassed driver quickly apologized and told me to hop in. When we got on the highway, he said partly to me, partly to himself, "It's a real war, eh?" And after taking a long breath, he added nostalgically, "Just like in the old days."

Now that "just like in the old days" keeps echoing in my mind, and I suddenly see this whole conflict with Lebanon in a completely different light. Thinking back, trying to re-create my conversations with worried friends about this war with Lebanon, about the Iranian missiles, the Syrian machinations, and the assumption that Hezbollah's leader, Sheikh Hassan Nasrallah, has the ability to strike any place in the country, even Tel Aviv, I realize that there was a small gleam in almost everyone's eyes, a kind of unconscious breath of relief.

And no, it's not that we Israelis long for war or death or grief, but we do long for those "old days" the taxi driver talked about. We long for a real war to take the place of all those exhausting years of intifada, when there was no black or white, only gray; when we were confronted not by armed forces, but only resolute young people wearing explosive belts; years when the aura of bravery ceased to exist, replaced by long lines of people waiting at our checkpoints, women about to give birth and elderly people struggling to endure the stifling heat.

Suddenly, the first salvo of missiles returned us to that familiar feeling of a war fought against a ruthless enemy who attacks our borders, a truly vicious enemy, not one fighting for its freedom and self-determination, not the kind that makes us stammer and throws us into confusion. Once again we're confident about the rightness of our cause, and we return with lightning speed to the bosom of the patriotism we had almost abandoned. Once again, we're a small country surrounded by enemies, fighting for our lives, not a strong, occupying country forced to fight daily against a civilian population.

So is it any wonder that we're all secretly just a tiny bit relieved? Give us Iran, give us a pinch of Syria, give us a handful of Sheikh Nasrallah, and we'll devour them whole. After all, we're no better than anyone else at resolving moral ambiguities. But we always did know how to win a war.

# Year Two

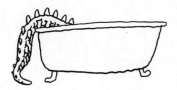

# Yours, Insincerely

When I was a kid, I always thought that Hebrew Book Week was a legitimate holiday, something that fit comfortably amid Independence Day, Passover, and Hanukkah. On this occasion, we didn't sit around campfires, spin dreidels, or hit each other on the head with plastic hammers, and, unlike other holidays, it doesn't commemorate a historical victory or heroic defeat, which made me like it even more.

At the beginning of every June, my sister, brother, and I would walk with our parents to the central square in Ramat Gan, where dozens of tables had been set up and covered in books. Each of us would choose five. Sometimes the author of one of those books would be at the table and would write a dedication in it. My sister really liked that. Personally, I found it a little annoying. Even if someone writes a book, it doesn't give him the right to scribble in my own private copy—especially if his handwriting is ugly, like a pharmacist's, and he insists on using hard words you have to look up in the dictionary, only to discover that all he really meant was "enjoy."

Years have passed, and even though I'm not a kid anymore, I still get just as excited during Book Week. But now the experience is a little different and a lot more stressful.

Before I started publishing books, I inscribed dedications only in those I bought to give as gifts to people I knew. Then one day I suddenly found myself signing books for people who'd bought them themselves, people I'd never met before. What can you write in the book of a total stranger who may be anything from a serial killer to a Righteous Gentile? "In friendship" borders on falsehood; "With admiration" doesn't hold water; "Best wishes" sounds too avuncular; and "Hope you enjoy my book!" oozes smarm from the first H to the final exclamation point. So, exactly eighteen years ago, on the last night of my first Book Week, I created my own genre: fictitious book dedications. If the books themselves are pure fiction, why should the dedications be true?

"To Danny, who saved my life on the Litani. If you hadn't tied that tourniquet, there'd be no me and no book."

"To Mickey. Your mother called. I hung up on her. Don't you dare show your face around here anymore."

"To Sinai. I'll be home late tonight, but I left some cholent in the fridge."

"To Feige. Where's that tenner I lent you? You said two days and it's a month already. I'm still waiting."

"To Tziki. I admit that I acted like a shit. But if your sister can forgive me, so can you."

"To Avram. I don't care what the lab tests show. For me, you'll always be my dad."

"Bosmat, even though you're with another guy now, we both know you'll come back to me in the end."

In retrospect, and after the slap in the face I got for that last one, I suppose I shouldn't have written what I did for the tall guy with the Marine buzz cut who was buying a book for his girlfriend, though I still think he could have made a civil remark instead of getting physical.

In any case, I learned my lesson, however painfully, and since then, during every Book Week, no matter how much my hand itches to write in the books bought by some Dudi or Shlomi that the next time he sees anything from me on paper it'll be a lawyer's letter, I take a deep breath and scribble "Best wishes" instead. Boring, maybe, but much easier on the face.

So, if that tall guy and Bosmat are reading this, I want them to know that I am truly repentant and would like to offer my belated apologies. And if by chance you're reading this, Feige, I'm still waiting for the tenner.

# Flight Meditation

A few months ago, I opened my rusty mailbox to find a blue-and-white envelope containing a gold plastic card embossed with my last name, and, above it, in flowery letters, *Frequent Flyer Club Gold*. I showed the card to my wife in a pathetic gesture, hoping that this sign of appreciation from an objective, outside party would soften her harsh opinion of me, but it didn't really work.

"I advise you not to show this card to anyone," she said.

"Why not?" I argued. "This card makes me a member of an exclusive club."

"Yes," my wife said, smiling that jackal smile of hers. "The exclusive club of people who have no life."

So, OK. In the discreet, intimate confines of this book, I am willing to make a partial admission that I don't have a life, at least not in the traditional, everyday sense of the word. And I admit that more than once in the past year I have had to read the stub of my plane ticket, which was nestled peacefully among the pages of my stamp-tattooed passport, to find out what country I was in. And I also admit that during those trips, which often followed a fifteen-hour flight, I found myself reading to a very small group of people who, after listening patiently to me for an hour, could offer only a consoling pat on the back and the hopeful observation that in Hebrew those stories of mine probably make sense. But I love it. I love reading to people: when they enjoy it, I enjoy it with them, and when they suffer, I figure it's probably coming to them.

The truth, now that I've launched into an inexplicable outburst of sincerity, is that I'm willing to confess I also love the flights themselves. Not the security checks before them or the sour-faced airline employees at the check-in counter who explain that the last empty seat left on the plane is between two flatulent Japanese sumo wrestlers. And I'm not really crazy about the endless waiting for luggage after landing, or the jet lag that digs a transatlantic tunnel through my skull with a particularly dull teaspoon. It's the middle I love, that part when you're closed up in a tin box that's floating between heaven and earth. A tin box that is totally cut off from the world, and inside it there's no real time or real weather, just a juicy slice of limbo that lasts from takeoff till landing.

And strangely enough, for me, those flights don't just mean eating the heated-up TV dinner that the sardonic copywriter for the airlines decided to call a "High Altitude Delight." They're a kind of meditative disengagement from the world. Flights are expansive moments when the phone doesn't ring and the Internet doesn't work. The maxim that flying time is wasted time liberates me from my anxieties and guilt feelings, and it strips me of all ambitions, leaving room for a different sort of existence. A happy, idiotic existence, the kind that doesn't try to make the most of time but is satisfied with merely finding the most enjoyable way to spend it.

The "I" who exists between takeoff and landing is a completely different person. The in-flight "I" is addicted to tomato juice, a drink I wouldn't think of touching when my feet are on the ground. In the air, that "I" avidly watches mind-numbing Hollywood comedies on a screen the size of a hemorrhoid and delves into the pages of the product catalog kept in the pocket of the seat in front of me as if it were an updated, upgraded version of the Old Testament.

I don't know if you've ever heard of the wallet made of rust-resistant steel fibers, material developed by NASA that guarantees that the bills inside will remain fresh long after our planet has been destroyed. Or the cat toilet that sucks out the smells and is camouflaged within a plant, providing your cat with full privacy while it's doing its thing, and preventing unpleasantness for household members and guests. Or the microprocessor-controlled antiseptic device that inserts antimicrobial silver ions into tissue with a budding infection in order to avert the disaster of an open sore. I've not only heard of all of these inventions but can also quote from memory the exact descriptions of each of those products, including the various colors they come in, as if they were verses from Ecclesiastes. After all, they didn't send me that Gold Card for nothing.

I'm writing this during a flight from Tel Aviv to Frankfurt on my way to Bangkok, and I'm doing it with very uncharacteristic speed so that, in another few lines, when it's finished, I can get comfortable in my seat again and browse through the in-flight magazine a little longer for an update on how many new destinations Lufthansa will be flying to soon. Then maybe I can catch the last fifteen minutes of *The Blind Side*, or go for some mingling on the line to the bathroom at the back of the plane. I have another hour and fourteen minutes till we land, and I want to make the most of them.

# Strange Bedfellows

The Swiss guy with the funny hat sitting next to me on the balcony of the Indus restaurant is sweating like crazy. I can't blame him. I'm sweating quite a bit too, and I'm supposed to be used to temperatures like this. But Bali isn't Tel Aviv. The air here is so damp that you can actually drink it with a straw. The Swiss guy tells me that he's between jobs now, which gives him time to travel. Not too long ago, he managed a resort hotel in New Caledonia, but he was fired. It's a long story, he says, but he'll be glad to tell it to me. The Turkish writer he's been trying to hit on all night told him she was going to the bathroom about an hour ago and still hasn't come back. He's already had so much to drink, he says, that if he tries to get up he'll probably roll down the stairs, so he's better-off sitting where he is, ordering another frozen vodka, and telling me his story.

He thought the idea of managing a resort in New Caledonia sounded cool. It wasn't till he got there that he realized what a hole-in-the-wall the place was. The air conditioners in the rooms didn't work, and there were insurgents in the nearby mountains who tended not to bother anyone, but for some inexplicable reason—probably boredom—liked to scare hotel guests who went out walking. The cleaning women categorically refused to go anywhere near the hotel's industrial washing machine, which they claimed was haunted, and they insisted on washing the sheets in the river instead. In short, the resort looked nothing like its brochure.

He'd been on the job for a month when a rich American couple arrived. From the minute they entered the small lobby, he had a feeling they were going to be trouble. They had that look of typical unsatisfied customers, the kind who come to the reception desk to complain about the temperature of the water in the pool. The Swiss guy sat behind the reception desk, poured himself a glass of whiskey, and waited for the couple's irate call. It came in less than fifteen minutes. "There's a lizard in the bathroom," shouted the hoarse voice on the other end of the line. "There are a lot of lizards on the island, sir," the Swiss guy said politely. "That's part of the charm of the place."

"The charm of the place?" the American yelled. "The charm of the place? My wife and I are not charmed. I want someone up here to get that lizard out of our room, do you hear me?"

"Sir," the Swiss guy said, "removing that particular lizard won't help. The area is full of lizards. There's a good chance that, by tomorrow morning, you'll find another few like it in your room, maybe even in your bed. But it's not that bad because—"

The Swiss guy didn't get to finish his sentence. The American had already slammed down the receiver. Here it comes, the Swiss guy thought as he gulped down the remains of his whiskey. In another minute they'd be at the reception desk yelling at him. With his luck, they probably knew some higher-up in the resort chain, and he'd be screwed.

He rose tiredly from behind the reception desk, having decided to take action: He'd get a bottle of champagne and bring it to them himself. He'd suck up to them the way they'd taught him in hotel management school and get himself out of this mess. It's no fun, but it's the right thing to do. Halfway to their room, he saw the Americans' car speeding toward him. It zipped past him, almost running him over, and continued in the direction of the main road. He tried to wave good-bye but the car didn't slow down.

He went to their room. They left the door open. Their bags were gone. He opened the door to the bathroom and saw the lizard. The lizard saw him, too. They looked at each other in silence for a few seconds. It was about five feet long and had claws. He'd seen one like it once, in some nature film, chewing on a live goat; he didn't remember exactly what the film had to say about them, only that they were very scary, unpleasant things. Now he understood why the Americans had taken off like that.

"And that's the end of the story," the Swiss guy said. It turns out that those Americans really did write a letter, and a week later, he was fired. He's been traveling around ever since. In November, he'll be going back to Switzerland to see if he can make it in his brother's business.

When I ask him if he thinks there's a moral to his story, he says he's sure there must be, but doesn't know exactly what it is. "Maybe," he says after a short pause, "it's that this world is full of lizards, and even though there's nothing we can do about it, it is always helpful to find out how big they are."

The Swiss guy asks me where I'm from. Israel, I tell him, and I had a hell of a time getting to this writers' festival. My parents didn't want me to come. They were afraid I'd be kidnapped here, or killed. After all, Indonesia is a Muslim country, and very anti-Israel, even anti-Semitic, some say. I tried to calm them down by sending them a link to a Wikipedia page that said Bali has a vast Hindu majority. It didn't help. Dad insisted that you don't need a majority vote to put a bullet in my head. Once Israeli flags were burned in front of the Israeli embassy in Jakarta, but since diplomatic relations were broken off, those flags had to be burned in front of the American embassy. A living, breathing Israeli could really make their day.

Getting a visa was a hassle, too—I had to wait five days in Bangkok, and I would've had to go back to Israel if the festival director hadn't managed to get to a senior official in the Indonesian Foreign Ministry through his Facebook page and become his Facebook friend. I tell the Swiss guy that in a little while, I'll be reading at the opening event in the Bali palace in front of the governor of the island and representatives of the royal family, and if he's able to stand on his feet by then, he's invited. The Swiss guy really likes the idea. I have to help him stand up, but after the first step, he manages to walk by himself.

There are more than five hundred people at the event. The

governor and representatives of the royal family are sitting in the first row. They look at me while I read. I can't really decipher their expressions, but they look very focused. I'm the first Israeli writer ever to come to Bali. I may even be the first Israeli, maybe even the first Jew, some members of the audience have ever seen. What do they see when they look at me? Probably a lizard, and from the smiles slowly spreading across their faces, this lizard is a lot smaller and more sociable than they expected.

# Defender of the People

There's nothing like a few days in eastern Europe to bring out the Jew in you. In Israel, you can walk around all day under the blazing sun in a sleeveless T-shirt and feel just like a goy: a little trance, a little opera, a good book by Bulgakov, a glass of Irish whiskey. But the minute they stamp your passport at the airport in Poland, you start to feel different. You might still be able to taste the flavor of your Tel Aviv life and God hasn't yet revealed himself to you in the broken fluorescent light flashing above you in the arrivals terminal, but with every whiff of pork, you feel increasingly like some kind of converso. You're surrounded, suddenly, by Diaspora.

From the day you were born in Israel, you've been taught that what happened in Europe over the past few centuries was nothing but a series of persecutions and pogroms, and despite the dictates of common sense, the lessons of that education continue to fester somewhere in your gut. It's an unpleasant feeling, somehow always affirmed by reality. Nothing grandiose happens—a Cossack doesn't rape your mother or your sister. It can be a seemingly innocent comment on the street, graffiti of a Star of David and some unclear slogan on a crumbling wall, the way the light reflects off the cross of the church opposite your hotel window, or a conversation between a couple of German tourists resonating against the background of the misty Polish countryside.

Then the questions begin: Is this truth or phobia? Are those semi-anti-Semitic events insinuating themselves into your mind because you anticipate them? My wife, for example, insists that I have superhuman power when it comes to detecting swastikas. It doesn't matter where we are—Melbourne, Berlin, or Zagreb—I can locate a swastika quicker than a Google map.

On my first trip to Germany as a writer, exactly fifteen years ago, my local publisher had invited me to an excellent Bavarian restaurant (I admit that sounds like an oxymoron), and just as our main course arrived, a tall, strapping German about sixty years old walked in and began to speak in a loud voice. His face was red and he looked drunk. From the jumble of German words he tossed into the air, I recognized only the two he kept repeating: *"Juden raus!"* I went over to the guy and said in English in a tone that tried to sound calm: "I'm a Jew. You want to take me out of here? Come on, do it, take me out." The German, who didn't understand a word of English, kept shouting in German, and in no time at all, we were in a shoving match. My publisher tried to intervene and asked me to go back and sit down.

"You don't understand," he tried to say. But I persisted. I understood very well. As second generation—the child of Holocaust survivors—I felt that I understood what was going on there better than any of the restaurant's calm patrons. At some point, the waiters pulled us apart, and the angry drunk was thrown out. I went back to the table. My food was cold, but I wasn't hungry anymore, anyway. While we were waiting for the check, my publisher explained in a deep, quiet voice that the furious drunk had been complaining that one of the diners' cars was blocking his vehicle. The words that had sounded to me like *Juden raus* were actually *jeden raus*, which translates roughly to "each out." When the check came, I insisted on paying. Reparations to a different Germany, if you will. What can I do? Even today, every other word of the German language puts me on the defensive.

But as they say, "Just because you're paranoid doesn't mean they're not after you." During the twenty years I've been traveling the world, I've collected a number of genuine anti-Semitic experiences that can't be explained away by a mistake in understanding.

There was, for instance, a Hungarian guy who met me in a local bar after a literary event in Budapest and insisted on showing me the giant German eagle tattooed on his back. He said that his grandfather killed three hundred Jews in the Holocaust, and he himself hoped to boast someday about a similar number.

In a small, peaceful East German town, a tipsy actor who had read some of my stories on stage two hours earlier explained to me that anti-Semitism is a terrible thing, but you can't deny that the intolerable behavior of the Jews throughout history helped fan the flames.

A clerk in a French hotel told me and the Arab Israeli writer Sayed Kashua that if it were up to him, his hotel wouldn't accept Jews. I spent the rest of the evening listening to Sayed's grumbling that on top of forty-two years of the Zionist occupation, he also has to bear the insult of being taken for a Jew.

And only a week ago, at a literary festival in Poland, someone in the audience asked me if I was ashamed to be a Jew. I gave him a logical, well-reasoned answer that wasn't the slightest bit emotional. The audience, which had listened attentively, applauded. But later, in my hotel room, I had a hard time falling asleep.

There's nothing like a couple of good November khamsins to put the Jew in you back in its place. The direct Middle Eastern sunlight burns all traces of the Diaspora right out of you. My best friend, Uzi, and I are sitting on Gordon Beach in Tel Aviv. Sitting next to him are Krista and Renate. "Don't tell me," Uzi says, trying to cover up his ballooning horniness with some unsuccessful telepathy. "You're both from Sweden."

"No," Renate says, laughing, "we're from Düsseldorf. Germany. You know Germany?"

"Sure," Uzi says, nodding enthusiastically, "Kraftwerk, Modern Talking, Nietzsche, BMW, Bayern München . . ." He forages around in his brain for a few more German associations, to no avail. "Hey, bro," he says to me, "why did we send you to college for all those years? How about contributing a little something to the conversation."

# Requiem for a Dream

I t all began with a dream. A lot of troubles in my life begin with a dream. And in this dream I was at a train station in a strange city, behind a hot dog stand. A horde of passengers were huddling around it. They were all jumpy, impatient. They were dying for a hot dog, they were afraid of missing the train. They were barking orders at me in a strange language that sounded like a scary blend of German and Japanese. I answered them in the same strange, nerve-wracking language. They tried to make me go faster, and I did my best to keep up. My shirt was so splattered with mustard and relish and sauerkraut that the few places where you could still see the white looked like spots. I tried to concentrate on the buns but couldn't help noticing the angry mob. They looked at me with the ravenous eyes of predators. The orders in the incomprehensible language seemed more and more menacing. My hands started to shake. Beads of salty sweat dripped from my forehead onto the thick hot dogs. And then I woke up.

The first time I had that dream was five years ago. In the middle of the night, when I got out of bed, covered in perspiration, I made do with a glass of iced tea and watched an episode of *The Wire*. It's not that I'd never had a bad dream before, but when I saw this one start to make itself at home in my unconscious, I knew I had a problem, one that even the winning combination of iced tea and Officer Jimmy McNulty couldn't solve.

Uzi, a well-known dream and hot dog buff, worked out its meaning in no time. "You're second generation," he said. "Your parents were forced to leave their country, their home, their natural social environment overnight. That unsettling experience filtered down from your parents' unsettled consciousness to yours, which was unsettled to begin with. On top of which, there's the unstable reality of our lives in the Middle East and your being a new father. Stir it all up and what do you get? A dream that includes all of those fears: of being uprooted, of arriving in a strange, alien place, of being forced to work at something unfamiliar or unsuitable. You've got it all."

"That makes sense," I told Uzi. "But what do I do to make sure that nightmare doesn't come back—see a psychologist?"

"That won't do you any good," he said. "What's the therapist going to tell you? That your parents weren't actually persecuted by Nazis, that there's no chance of Israel being destroyed, leaving you a refugee? That even with your lousy coordination you can do a good job selling hot dogs? What you need isn't a bunch of lies from a PhD in clinical psych. You need a real solution: a nest egg in a foreign bank account. Everybody's doing it. I just read in the paper that foreign accounts, foreign passports, and four-wheel drives are the three official trends this summer."

"And that will work?" I asked.

"Like a charm," Uzi promised. "It'll help the dream and the reality. It's not going to keep you from becoming a refugee or anything, but at least you'll be a refugee with a bundle. The kind who even if he winds up with a hot dog stand at a train station in Japa-Germany has enough cash to hire another refugee with even lousier luck to stand there and stuff the sauerkraut."

Taking advantage of refugees wasn't an idea that appealed to me at first, but after a few more nocturnal visits to the hot dog stand, I decided to go for it. On the Internet, I managed to find a nice website of an Australian bank, with a promotional video that showed not only breathtaking landscapes but a smiling teller, who looked like Julia Roberts's even nicer sister and urged me to deposit my money with them.

Uzi nixed the idea straightaway. "Ten years from now Australia won't even be there. If the hole in the ozone layer doesn't get to them, the Chinese takeover will. It's a sure thing. My cousin works in the Mossad, Pacific Division. Go for Europe. Any place except Russia and Switzerland."

"What's the problem there?"

"The Russian economy is unstable," Uzi explained, taking a big bite of falafel. "And the Swiss . . . I dunno. I don't like them. They're kind of cold, if you know what I mean."

Eventually I found a nice bank in the Channel Islands. Truth is, before I started looking for a bank I didn't even know there were islands in the Channel. And it may well be that even in the worst-case scenario of a world war, the bad guys who'll conquer the world won't realize there are islands there, either, and that even under global occupation, my bank will stay free. The guy at the bank who agreed to take my money was named Jeffrey but insisted that I call him Jeff. A year later he was replaced by someone named John or Joe, and then there was a very nice new guy named Jack. All of them were pleasant and polite, and when they talked about my stocks and bonds and their secure future they made sure to use the present perfect tense correctly, something that Uzi and I never managed to do. Which only reassured me more.

All around me, squabbles in the Middle East were growing more aggressive. Hezbollah's Grad missiles were hitting Haifa, and Hamas rockets were thrashing buildings in Ashdod. But despite the deafening explosions, I slept like a baby. And it wasn't that I didn't have any dreams, but what I dreamed about was the pastoral setting of a bank, surrounded by water, and Jeffrey or John or Jack taking me there in a gondola. The view from the gondola was dazzling, and flying fish swam along with us, singing to me in a human voice that sounded a bit like Celine Dion's about the splendor and beauty of my investment portfolio, which was growing by the minute. According to Uzi's Excel charts, it had grown to the point where I could open at least two hot dog stands or, if I preferred, one roofed kiosk.

And then came October 2008, and the fish in my dream stopped singing. After the market crashed, I called Jason, who had replaced the last J on the list, and asked him if he thought I ought to sell. He said I'd do better to wait. I don't remember just how he said it, except that he, too, like all the J's before him, made very correct use of the present perfect. Two weeks later, my money was worth another thirty percent less. In my dreams, the bank still looked the same, but the gondola had begun capsizing and the flying fish, which didn't look the least bit friendly anymore, started talking to me in the same familiar Japo-German dialect. Even if I'd wanted to, I couldn't have bribed them with a good hot dog. Uzi's Excel charts left no doubt that I could barely afford a warm coat and a pair of shoes. I kept phoning the bank. In our first few conversations, Jason sounded optimistic. Then he began getting defensive and, at a certain point, simply indifferent. When I asked him if he was looking at my investments and trying to do something to salvage what was left of them, he explained the bank's policy: proactive management began with portfolios of one million dollars and up. I knew then we'd never again take a gondola trip together.

"Look at the bright side," Uzi said, and pointed at the picture of a friendly-looking man in the newspaper's financial supplement. "At least you didn't invest your money with Madoff." As for Uzi, he made it through the crisis unscathed; he gambled all his money on wheat crops in India or weapons in Angola or vaccines in China. Before that conversation, I'd never heard of Madoff, but now I know all about Bernie. In retrospect, apart from the bit about the rip-off, we have a lot in common: two restless Jews who love to make up stories and have been sailing along for years in a gondola with a hole in the bottom. Did he, too, once, years ago, dream he was selling hot dogs at the train station? Maybe he also had some true friend, like Uzi, who never stopped giving bum advice?

The guy on the news just announced a state of alert in the middle of the country and that there are roadblocks on some of the highways. There are rumors about a soldier being abducted. On my way home I buy a pack of diapers for Lev and stop at the video store to pick up a few episodes of *The Wire* and a bottle of iced tea. Just to be on the safe side.

# Long View

The pleasant-voiced captain apologizes again over the loud-speaker. The plane was scheduled to take off two hours earlier and we still haven't left. "Our crew still hasn't been able to determine the problem with the plane, so we need to ask our passengers to disembark. We will update you as soon as we can."

The skinny young guy sitting next to me says, "It's me. I did it. When we got on the plane, I talked to my wife on my cell, remember? She told me she was on the way to the beach with our daughter and the baby. I'm sitting here with my safety belt buckled, and all I can think is, Why the hell am I going to Italy? Instead of spending Saturday with my wife and daughter, why am I flying six hours, including a connecting flight, for some hourlong meeting my boss said was important? I hope the plane breaks down. I swear, that's what I thought, I hope the plane breaks down, and look what happened."

As we reenter the terminal, a big woman wearing a flowered

dress and dragging a suitcase the size of a coffin goes up to the skinny guy and asks him where we're coming from. "Who cares where we're coming from"—he winks at me—"the main thing is where we're headed."

A few hours later, when I get on the small, crowded replacement plane that will take me to Rome on my way to Sicily, I'll walk down the aisle and notice that the skinny guy isn't there. Throughout the flight, I'll picture him on the beach in Tel Aviv building sand castles with his wife and kid, and I'll be jealous.

I also have a wife, and a little boy, waiting for me in Tel Aviv. From the start, this trip was really inconvenient for me, too, and with every minute of delay it's becoming less desirable. On Saturday evening I'm supposed to take part in an event at a small book festival in the town of Taormina. When the organizers invited me, I agreed to go because I thought I could take my family along, but a few weeks ago my wife realized that she had a prior work commitment, and I was stuck with my own promise to attend the festival. The trip, originally planned for a week, was shortened to two days, and now it turns out that, as a result of the supernatural powers of a skinny young guy who wanted to play with his kid, half of those two days will be wasted in airports.

Because of the delay, I miss my connecting flight from Rome to Catania, in Sicily. When I finally make it to the island, it's another long ride to Taormina, and by the time I arrive at the hotel, it's already dark. A mustached reception clerk gives me the key to my room. Lying asleep on a small couch in the lobby is a cute little boy, about seven, who looks just like the reception clerk, minus the mustache. I climb into bed with all my clothes on and fall asleep.

The night goes by in a long, dark, dreamless instant, but the morning makes up for it. I open the window to find that I'm in a dream: Stretched out before me is a gorgeous landscape of beach and stone houses. A long walk and a few conversations in broken English punctuated with a lot of enthusiastic arm waving reinforce the unreal feel of the place. After all, I know this sea very well; it's the same Mediterranean that's only a five-minute walk from my house in Tel Aviv, but the peace and tranquillity projected by the locals here are something I have never encountered before. The same sea, but without the frightening, black, existential cloud I'm used to seeing hanging over it. Maybe this is what Shimon Peres meant back in those innocent days when he talked about "a new Middle East."

This is Taormina's first book festival. The people on the organizing team are extremely nice, and the atmosphere is relaxed; this festival seems to have everything except an audience at the events. Not that I'm passing judgment on the city's residents: When you're in the heart of a paradise like this, in the middle of a hot July, would you rather spend the day at one of the most beautiful beaches in the world or in a mosquito-riddled public garden having your mind numbed by a wild-haired writer speaking strangely accented English?

But in the harmonious atmosphere of Taormina, even a small audience isn't considered a failure. I think that these pleasant people, who speak such a lovely, melodious Italian and live in such gorgeous surroundings, would accept even boils and plagues with an understanding smile. After the event, the mild-mannered English translator points to the dark sea and tells me that during the day you can see the Italian mainland from here. "You see those lights there?" he asks, pointing toward a few flickering pinpoints. "That's Reggio Calabria, the southernmost city in Italy."

When I was a kid, my parents used to tell me bedtime stories. During World War II, the stories their parents told them were never read from books because there were no books to be had, so they made up their own. As parents themselves, they continued that tradition, and from a very young age, I felt a special pride, because the bedtime stories I heard every night couldn't be bought in any store; they were mine alone. My mother's stories were always about dwarves and fairies, while my father's were about the time he lived in southern Italy, from 1946 to 1948.

His fellow members of the Irgun wanted him to try to buy weapons for them, and after asking around and pulling a few strings, my father found himself at the southernmost tip of Italy, from which you can see the Sicilian coast—Reggio Calabria. There he rubbed shoulders with the local Mafia and, in the end, persuaded them to sell him rifles for the Irgun to use to fight the British. Since he had no money to rent an apartment, the local Mafia offered him free lodgings in a whorehouse they owned there, and that, it seems, was the best time of his life.

The heroes of my father's bedtime stories were always drunks and prostitutes, and as a child, I loved them very much. I didn't know yet what a drunk and a prostitute were, but I did recognize magic, and my father's bedtime stories were filled with magic and compassion. Now, forty years later, here I am, not far from the world of my childhood stories. I try to imagine my father coming here after the war, nineteen years old at the time, to this place that, despite its many troubles and dark alleys, projects such a sense of peace and tranquillity. Compared with the horrors and cruelty he witnessed during the war, it's easy to imagine how his new acquaintances from the underworld must have appeared to him: happy, even compassionate. He walks down the street, smiling faces wish him a good day in mellifluous Italian, and for the first time in his adult life, he doesn't have to be afraid or hide the fact that he's a Jew.

When I try to reconstruct those bedtime stories my father told me years ago, I realize that beyond their fascinating plots, they were meant to teach me something. Something about the almost desperate human need to find good in the least likely places. Something about the desire not to beautify reality but to persist in searching for an angle that would put ugliness in a better light and create affection and empathy for every wart and wrinkle on its scarred face. And here, in Sicily, sixty-three years after my father left it, as I face a few dozen pairs of riveted eyes and a lot of empty plastic chairs, that mission suddenly seems more possible than ever.

# Year Three

# Throwdown at
# the Playground

I don't want to brag, but I've managed to earn myself a unique, somewhat mythic status among the parents who take their children to Ezekiel Park, my son's favorite spot in Tel Aviv. I attribute that special achievement not to any overwhelming charisma I may possess, but rather to two common, lackluster qualities: I'm a man, and I'm hardly ever working. In Ezekiel Park, I have been dubbed *ha-abba*, or "the father," an almost religious and slightly gentile nickname intoned with great respect by all the park's regulars. Most of the fathers in my neighborhood go off to work every morning, so the inherent laziness that has plagued me for so many years is finally being construed as exceptional sensitivity and affection, a genuine understanding for children's tender young souls.

As "the father," I can take an active part in conversations on a wide variety of subjects that until recently were alien to me, and I can expand my knowledge of topics such as nursing, breast pumps, and the relative merits of cloth diapers versus their disposable counterparts. There is something almost perversely soothing about discussing such things. As a stressed-out Jew who considers his momentary survival to be exceptional and not the least bit trivial, and whose daily Google Alerts are confined to the narrow territory between "iranian nuclear development" and "jews+genocide," there is nothing more enjoyable than a few tranquil hours spent discussing sterilizing bottles with organic soap and the red-pink rashes on a baby's bottom. But this week, the magic ended and political reality stealthily crept its way into my private paradise.

"Tell me something," Orit, the mother of three-year-old Ron, asked innocently. "Will Lev go to the army when he grows up?" The question caught me totally off guard. Over the last three years, I have had to deal with quite a few speculative questions about my son's future, but most were of the annoying but non-threatening would-you-advise-him-to-be-an-artist-even-though-from-the-way-you're-dressed-there-can't-be-much-money-in-it kind. But that question about the army thrust me into a different, surreal world in which I saw dozens of sturdy babies swathed in environmentally friendly cloth diapers sweeping down from the mountains on miniature ponies, weapons brandished in their pink hands, shouting murderous battle cries. And facing them, alone, stands chubby little Lev, wearing scruffy fatigues and an army vest. A green steel helmet, slightly too large, slides over his eyes, as he clutches a bayoneted rifle in his tiny hands. The first wave of diapered riders has almost reached him. He presses the rifle against his shoulder and closes one eye to aim. . . .

"So what do you say?" Orit awakened me from my unpleasant reverie. "Are you going to let him serve in the army or not? Don't tell me you haven't talked about it yet." There was something accusing in her tone, as if the fact that my wife and I haven't discussed our baby's military future is on the same scale as skipping his measles vaccination. I refused to give in to the guilt feelings that come so naturally to me and replied unhesitatingly, "No, we haven't talked about it. We still have time. He's three years old."

"If you feel that you still have time, then take it," Orit snapped back sarcastically. "Assaf and I have already made up our minds about Ron. He's not going into the army."

That night, sitting in front of the TV news, I told my wife about the strange incident in Ezekiel Park. "Isn't that weird," I said, "talking about recruiting a kid who still can't put on his underpants by himself?"

"It's not weird at all," my wife replied. "It's natural. All the mothers in the park talk to me about it."

"So how come they haven't said anything to me about it till now?"

"Because you're a man."

"So what if I'm a man," I argue. "They have no problem talking to me about nursing."

"Because they know you'll be understanding and empathetic about nursing, but you'll just be snide when it comes to serving in the army."

"I wasn't snide," I defended myself. "I just said that it's a strange subject to be dealing with when the kid's so young."

"I've been dealing with it from the day Lev was born," my wife confessed. "And if we're already discussing it now, I don't want him to go into the army."

I was silent. Experience has taught me that there are some situations in which it's better to keep quiet. That is, I tried to keep quiet. Life gives me good advice, but sometimes I refuse to take it. "I think it's very controlling to say something like that," I finally said. "After all, in the end, he'll have to decide those things by himself."

"I'd rather be controlling," my wife answered, "than have to take part in a military funeral on the Mount of Olives fifteen years from now. If it's controlling to keep your son from putting his life at risk, then that's exactly what I am."

At that point, the argument heated up and I turned off the TV. "Listen to yourself," I said. "You're talking as if serving in the army is an extreme sport. But what can we do? We live in a part of the world where our lives depend on it. So what you're actually saying is that you'd rather have other people's children go into the army and sacrifice their lives, while Lev enjoys his life here without taking any risks or shouldering the obligations the situation calls for."

"No," my wife responded. "I'm saying that we could have reached a peaceful solution a long time ago, and we still can. And that our leaders allow themselves not to do that because they know that most people are like you: they won't hesitate to put their children's lives into the government's irresponsible hands."

I was about to answer her when I sensed another pair of huge eyes watching me. Lev was standing at the entrance to the living room. "Daddy," he asked, "why are you and Mommy fighting?"

"We are not really fighting." I tried to come up with something. "This isn't a real fight, it is just a drill."

Since that conversation with Orit, none of the mothers in the park have spoken to me again about Lev's military service. But I still can't get that image of him in uniform, armed with a rifle, out of my mind. Just yesterday, in the sandbox, I saw him push Orit's peacenik son Ron, and later, on the way home, he chased a cat with a stick. "Start saving, Daddy," I tell myself. "Start saving for a defense attorney. You're not raising just a soldier here, but a potential war criminal." I'd be happy to share those thoughts with my wife, but after we barely survived that last clash, I don't want to start a new one.

We managed to end our argument with an agreement of sorts. First, I suggested what sounded like a fair settlement: when the kid is eighteen, we'll let him decide for himself. But my wife rejected that out of hand, claiming he would never be able to make a really free choice with all the social pressure around him. In the end, out of exhaustion, and in the absence of any other solution, we decided to compromise on the only principle we both truly agreed on: to spend the next fifteen years working toward family and regional peace.

# Swede Dreams

**M**y visit last week to the Gothenburg Book Fair in Sweden got off to a stressful start. Several weeks before I arrived in that peaceful city, which boasts northern Europe's largest amusement park, a local tabloid published a story accusing Israel of harvesting organs from Palestinians killed by the IDF. The story managed to make an impressive quantum leap in logic by linking an unproven accusation against the Israeli army for something it had allegedly done in the early 1990s to a New Jersey rabbi accused of trafficking in human organs in 2009, as if the gap of more than a decade and thousands of miles were merely a trivial detail. The only thing missing in the article was a recipe for matzos made with the blood of Christian children.

The absurd report received a no less absurd response from the Israeli government, which demanded that the Swedish prime minister apologize for the story. The Swedes refused, of course, claiming freedom of the press, even if in this specific case, the press was not of particularly high quality. And Israel responded immediately with the unconventional weapon it keeps hidden away for conflicts of just such magnitude: a consumer boycott of IKEA. In the midst of this hyperventilated political storm, yours truly found himself spending Rosh Hashanah with an audience of polite Swedish readers who generously thanked him for his stories but also kept an eye open while he autographed their books to make sure he didn't take advantage of the moment to snatch a kidney or two.

But my real Swedish drama began when I realized there was a danger that I might not get back to Israel before Yom Kippur. Over the past few years, I've spent quite a few holidays outside of Israel, and despite the self-pitying, whiny face I always present to people around me, I have to admit I've often felt somewhat relieved to spend an Independence Day without an aerial demonstration of air force planes right over my head, or a Shavuot eve minus aunts and uncles who are insulted because I've refused their invitations to a holiday dinner. But I always did everything I could to be in Israel on Yom Kippur. All these years, all my life.

The night after the problem of my flight back was solved—with the help of my host's savvy travel agent—I invited everyone to celebrate our success at a local Swedish restaurant called, for some reason, Cracow, which is famous, of course, for its huge selection of Czech beers. "Now that it's all been worked out, maybe you can explain to us what the hell is so special about that holiday," my young Swedish publisher asked. And so

I found myself, with a stomach full of cold potato salad and draft beer, trying to explain to a few half-drunk literary Swedes what Yom Kippur is.

The Swedes listened and were fascinated. The thought of a day when no motorized vehicles drive through the cities, when people walk around without their wallets and all the stores are closed, when there are no TV broadcasts or even updates on websites, to them sounded more like an innovative Naomi Klein concept than an ancient Jewish holiday. The fact that it was also a day when you're supposed to ask others for forgiveness and do moral stocktaking upgraded the anti-consumerist angle with a welcome touch of '60s hippiedom. And the fasting bit sounded like an extreme version of the fashionable low-carb diet they'd talked to me about in such glowing terms just that morning. And so I began the evening trying to explain the ancient Hebrew ritual in my broken English, and found myself doing PR for the coolest, most sought-after holiday in the universe, the iPhone of all festivals.

At that point, the amazed Swedes were consumed by envy of me for having been born into such a wonderful religion. Their eyes darted around the restaurant, looking at the patrons as if they were searching for a mohel who would cut them a deal to join up.

Twenty-six hours later, I was strolling with my wife down the center lane of one of Tel Aviv's busiest thoroughfares, our little son behind us, riding his bike with the training wheels. Above us, birds were chirping their morning birdsong. I've spent my whole adult life on that street, but only on Yom Kippur do I get to hear the birds.

"Daddy," my son asked as he pedaled and panted, "tomorrow's Yom Kippur too, right?"

"No, son," I said, "tomorrow's a regular day."

He burst into tears.

I stood in the middle of the street watching the kid cry. "C'mon," my wife whispered to me, "say something to him."

"There's nothing to be said, love," I whispered back. "The child is right."

# Matchstick War

When the fighting in Gaza began last month, I found myself with a lot of spare time. The university in Beersheba where I teach was within the range of missiles fired by Hamas, and they had to close it. But after a couple of weeks, it reopened, and the next day I found myself taking an hour-and-a-half train ride from Tel Aviv, where I live, to Beersheba again. Half the students weren't there—mainly the ones who commuted from the center of the country—but the other half, the Beersheba locals, showed up. The bombs were dropping on them in any case, and conventional wisdom among the students was that the university's classrooms were better protected than their dorms and housing projects.

While I was having my coffee at the cafeteria, the bomb-shelter alarm started blaring outside. There wasn't time to get to a proper shelter, so I ran with some other people into the thick-walled, almost windowless entrance of a university building nearby. Around me were a few frightened students and a grave-faced lecturer who went on eating his sandwich on the concrete steps as if nothing were happening. A couple of the students said they'd heard an explosion in the distance, so it was probably safe to leave, but the lecturer, his mouth still full, pointed out that sometimes they shoot more than one missile and that we'd be better off waiting a few more minutes. While I was there, I recognized Kobi, a crazy kid from my childhood in Ramat Gan who liked fifth grade so much he stayed in it for two years.

At forty-two, Kobi looked exactly the same. It's not that he looked especially young; it's just that, even in elementary school, he seemed to be approaching middle age: a thick, hairy neck; powerful body; high forehead; and the smiling yet tough expression of an aging child who had already learned a thing or two about this stupid world. In retrospect, the malicious rumor among the kids at school that he was already shaving was probably true.

"Well, what do you know?" Kobi said, hugging me. "You haven't changed a bit," adding, by way of accuracy, "even the same height, just like elementary school."

Kobi and I caught up a bit, and after a while people around us felt safe enough to start making their way out of the protected space, leaving it for us. "That rocket was a stroke of luck," Kobi said. "Just think: If it wasn't for that Qassam rocket, we could have walked right past each other and never met."

Kobi said he didn't live nearby. He came to sniff around. Now that Beersheba's in rocket range, it has opened up quite a few real estate possibilities. Land values will drop; the state will hand out extra construction permits. In short, an entrepreneur who plays his cards right can find great opportunities.

The last time we met was almost twenty years ago. There were missiles then, too—Scuds that Saddam Hussein rained down on Ramat Gan. Kobi was still living at home. I'd gone back to be with my stubborn parents, who refused to leave the city. Kobi took our friend Uzi and me to his parents' apartment and showed us what he referred to as his Weapon and Matchstick Museum. There, on the walls of his childhood bedroom, hung an impressive collection of weaponry: swords, pistols, even flails. Beneath them stood a huge Eiffel Tower and a life-size guitar he had made out of matchsticks. He explained to us that the museum had originally been devoted to weapons alone, but after he was convicted of stealing grenades for the exhibition, he took advantage of his eight-month sentence to build the Eiffel Tower and the guitar and added them to the collection.

In those days, he was especially worried that an Iraqi missile strike would shatter the Eiffel Tower, on which he'd spent most of his jail time. Today, his matchstick creations are still at his parents' place, but Ramat Gan is outside the effective range of the missiles and rockets. "As far as the matchstick Eiffel Tower goes," Kobi said, "my situation over the last twenty years has definitely improved. I have my doubts about the rest."

On the train from Beersheba I read a paper someone had left behind on a seat. There was an item about the lions and ostriches at the Gaza Zoo. They were suffering from the bombing and hadn't been fed regularly since the war began. A brigade commander wanted to carry out a special operation to rescue one particular lion and transfer it to Israel. Another, smaller, item, without a picture, reported that the number of children who had died in the bombing of Gaza so far had passed three hundred. Like the ostriches, the rest of the children there would also have to fend for themselves. Our situation at the level of the matchstick Eiffel Tower has indeed improved beyond recognition. As for the rest, like Kobi, I have my doubts.

# Idol Worship

When I was three, I had a ten-year-old brother, and deep in my heart I hoped that when I grew up, I'd be just like him. Not that I stood a chance. My big brother had already skipped two grades and had an enviable understanding of everything, from atomic physics and computer programming to the Cyrillic alphabet. Around that time, my brother began to develop a serious concern about me. An article he read in *Haaretz* said that illiterate people are excluded from the job market, and it bothered him very much that his beloved three-year-old brother would have a hard time finding work. So he began to teach me reading and writing using a unique technique he called "the chewing gum method." It worked as follows: My brother would point to a word, which I had to read out loud. If I read it properly, he would give me a piece of unchewed gum. If I made a mistake, he stuck his chewed gum in my hair. The method worked like magic, and at the age of four, I was the only kid in nursery school who knew how to read. I was also the only kid who, at least at first glance, looked like he was balding. But that's another story.

When I was five, I had a twelve-year-old brother who found God and went to a religious boarding school, and deep in my heart I hoped that when I grew up, I'd be just like him. He used to talk to me a lot about religion. And I thought the midrashim he told me were the coolest things in the world. He was the youngest pupil in the school—because of all that grade-skipping he did—but everyone admired him. Not because he was so smart—somehow, that was less important in the boarding school—but because he was so good-natured and helpful. I remember visiting him one Purim, and every pupil we met thanked him for something else: one for helping him study for a test, another for fixing a transistor so he could listen secretly to heavy metal, still another for lending him a pair of sneakers before an important soccer game. He walked around that place like a king who was so modest and dreamy that he didn't even know he was regal, and I followed in his wake like a prince all too aware of his royalty. I remember thinking then that the whole business of believing in God would be part of my future, too. After all, my brother knew everything, and if he believed in the Creator, then there had to be one.

When I was eight, I had a fifteen-year-old brother who left religion and went to college to study mathematics and computer science, and deep in my heart I hoped that when I grew up, I'd be just like him. He lived in an apartment with his bespectacled girlfriend, who was twenty-four, an age that, from my childish perspective, seemed ancient. They used to kiss and drink beer and smoke cigarettes, and I was sure that if I played my cards right, in another seven years, I'd be there too. I'd sit on the grass at Bar-Ilan University and eat grilled cheese sandwiches from the cafeteria. I'd have a bespectacled girlfriend, and she'd kiss me, tongue and all. What could be better than that?

When I was fourteen, I had a twenty-one-year-old brother who fought in the Lebanon War. Lots of my classmates had brothers who fought in that war. But mine was the only one I knew who wasn't in favor of it. Even though he was a soldier, he never thrilled to the idea of shooting guns and throwing grenades, and especially not to the need to kill the enemy. Most of the time, he did what he was told, and the rest of the time he spent in military courts. When he was tried and found guilty of "behavior unbecoming an IDF soldier" after he turned an aerial antenna into a giant totem pole with a head and eagle's wings, my sister and I sneaked into the remote base in the Negev where he was confined. We spent hours playing cards with him and another soldier, Mosco, who was also confined, but for slightly less creative reasons. And as I watched my brother in his army pants, his torso bare, paint a watercolor picture of the wadi that ran below the base, I knew that that's just what I wanted to be when I grew up: a soldier who, even in uniform, never forgets his free spirit.

Years have passed since I sneaked onto my brother's base. In that time, he managed to get married and divorced, and married again. He also managed to work at successful high-tech companies and leave them so that he could dedicate himself, together with his second wife, to the kinds of social and political activities that reporters like to call "radical"—things like fighting against biometric records and police brutality and for human rights and legalizing marijuana. In that time, I have also managed to grow and change so that, apart from the love we've always felt for each other, the only constant in our relationship has been the seven-year difference between us. Throughout that long journey, I never got to be more than just a little of what my brother was, and at some point I guess I even stopped trying. Partly because my brother's strange route was a very difficult one to follow and partly because I've had my own personal crises and confusions to deal with.

For the past five years, my big brother and his wife have lived in Thailand. They build Internet sites for Israeli and international organizations that are trying to make our world a little bit better, and with the modest fee they get for their work, they manage to live very well in their cozy apartment in the town of Trat. They don't even have an air conditioner, a bathtub, or a toilet with running water, but they do have lots of good friends and neighbors who make the most delicious food in the world and are always happy to visit or host them. Four weeks ago, my wife, Lev, and I flew to see their new home. While we were there, we took an elephant tour, and on it my brother's elephant was a few steps in front of mine. Both were being driven by experienced Thais. After we had gone a few hundred yards, I saw my brother's driver signal that my brother should take over leading their animal. The Thai man moved to sit to the rear of the elephant and my brother began taking charge. He didn't yell at it or kick it lightly the way the local driver had done. He just bent forward and whispered something in the elephant's ear. From where I was sitting, it looked as if the elephant nodded and turned in the direction my brother wanted. And at that moment it came back to me—the feeling I'd had throughout my childhood and teenage years. That pride in my big brother and the hope that when I grew up, I'd be a little bit like him, able to drive elephants through virgin forests without ever having to raise my voice.

# Year Four

# Bombs Away

A few weeks before our son, Lev, was born, almost four years ago, two weighty philosophical issues came to the fore.

The first, will he look like his mom or his dad, was resolved quickly and unequivocally at his birth: he was beautiful. Or, as my dear wife so aptly puts it, "The only thing he inherited from you is the hair on his back."

And the second issue, what will he be when he grows up, was of concern for the first three years of his life. His bad temper qualified him to be a taxi driver; his phenomenal ability to make excuses indicated that he might do well in the legal profession; and his consistent mastery over others showed his potential to be a high-ranking member of one totalitarian government or another. But during the past few months the fog surrounding our son's plump and rosy future has begun to lift. He'll probably be a milkman, because if not, his rare ability to wake up every morning at five-thirty and insist on waking us, too, would go completely to waste.

One Wednesday, two weeks ago, our routine of being awakened at five-thirty a.m. was preempted by the doorbell. Dressed in my pajama bottoms, I opened the door and saw Uzi standing there, white as a sheet. Out on the balcony, he smoked nervously and told me that he'd had dinner with S., a crazy kid who'd gone to elementary school with us and had become, of course, a crazy high-ranking military officer. Around dessert, after Uzi finished bragging about a dubious real estate deal he'd just closed, S. told him about a secret dossier that had reached his desk. It dealt with the psychological makeup of the Iranian president. According to the dossier, which had originated in foreign-intelligence agencies, Mahmoud Ahmadinejad is one of the few living leaders in the world whose real views, aired only behind closed doors, are even more fanatical than the ones aired in public.

"It's almost always the opposite," S. had explained. "World leaders are barking dogs who don't bite. But with him, it seems, his desire to wipe Israel off the face of the earth is really a lot stronger than he actually says. And as you know, he says it quite a bit."

"Do you get it?" Uzi asked, covered in sweat. "That crazy Iranian is prepared to destroy Israel even if it means the total annihilation of Iran, because from a pan-Islamic perspective, he sees that as a victory. And in a few months, that guy is going to have a nuclear bomb. A nuclear bomb! Do you understand what a disaster it'll be for me if he drops it on Tel Aviv? I rent out fourteen apartments here. Did you ever hear of a radioactive mutation that pays its rent on time?"

"Get a hold of yourself, Uzi," I said. "You're not the only one who'll suffer if we get bombed. I mean, we have a kid here and—"

"A kid doesn't pay rent," Uzi yelled. "A kid doesn't sign a lease with you that he'll break without a second thought the minute he grows a third eye."

"Uncle Uzi," I heard Lev's sleepy voice behind me, "can I have a third eye, too?" At that point in the conversation, I also lit a cigarette.

The next day, when my wife asked me to call in a plumber to check a wet spot on the bedroom ceiling, I told her about my conversation with Uzi. "If S. is right," I said, "it would be a waste of our time and money. Why fix anything if the whole city is going to be wiped out in two months?" I suggested that maybe we should give it half a year, and if we're still here in one piece in March, we'll repair the ceiling then. My wife didn't say anything, but from her look I could tell that she hadn't realized the seriousness of the current geopolitical situation.

"So if I understand you correctly, you probably want to postpone the work on the garden, too?" she asked. I nodded. Why waste the citrus tree saplings and the violets we'd plant? According to the Internet, they're particularly sensitive to radiation.

Aided by Uzi's intelligence, I managed to save us from quite a few chores. The only home-repair job I agreed to take part in was roach extermination, because even radioactive fallout won't stop those pests. Gradually, my wife also began to realize the advantages of our shabby existence. After she found a not exactly reliable news site warning that Iran might already have nuclear weapons, she decided it was time to stop washing dishes. "There's nothing more frustrating than getting nuked while you're putting the soap in the dishwasher," she explained. "From now on, we only wash the dishes on an immediate-need basis."

This "If I'm going up in flames anyway, then I won't go as a sucker" philosophy extended well beyond the dishwasher edict. We quickly stopped unnecessary floor mopping and garbage removal. At my wife's cunning suggestion, we went straight to the bank to apply for a huge loan, figuring that if we take out the money fast enough, we can screw the system. "Let them come looking for us to pay it back when this country turns into a giant hole in the ground." We laughed as we sat in our filthy living room, watching our enormous new plasma TV. It would be nice if only once in our short lives we could really put one over on the bank.

And then one night I had a nightmare in which Ahmadinejad came over to me on the street, hugged me, kissed me on both cheeks, and said in fluent Yiddish, *"Ich hub dir lieb"*—My brother, I love you. I woke my wife. Her face was covered in plaster. The problem of the wet spot on the ceiling over our bed was getting worse. "What's wrong?" she asked, frightened. "Is it the Iranians?"

I nodded, but quickly reassured her that it was only in a dream.

"That they annihilated us?" she asked, stroking my cheek. "I have one of those every night."

"Even worse," I said. "I dreamed we were making peace with them."

That hit her really hard. "Maybe S. was wrong," she whispered in terror. "Maybe the Iranians won't attack. And we'll be stuck with this filthy, run-down apartment, with the debts and your students, whose papers you promised to give back by January and haven't even started to mark. And with those nudnik relatives of yours in Eilat we promised to visit for Pesach because we were sure that by then—"

"It was just a dream," I said, trying to cheer her up. "He's a lunatic, you can see it in his eyes." But that was too little, too late. I hugged her as hard as I could, letting her tears flow onto my neck, and whispered, "Don't worry, honey. We're both survivors. We've already survived quite a bit together—illnesses, wars, terrorist attacks, and, if peace is what fate has in store, we'll survive it, too." Finally my wife fell asleep again, but I couldn't. So I got up and swept the living room. First thing tomorrow morning, I'm calling a plumber.

# What Does the Man Say?

The minute we got into the taxi, I had a bad feeling. And it wasn't because the driver impatiently asked me to buckle the kid's safety belt in the backseat after I'd already done so, or because he muttered something that sounded like a curse when I said we wanted to go to Ramat Gan. I take a lot of taxis, so I'm used to the bad tempers, the impatience, the armpit sweat stains. But there was something about the way that driver spoke, something half violent and half on the verge of tears that made me uncomfortable. Lev was almost four then, and we were on our way to Grandma's. Unlike me, he couldn't have cared less about the driver and focused mainly on the tall, ugly buildings that kept smiling at him along the way. He sang "Yellow Submarine" quietly to himself with words he made up that sounded almost like English, and waved his short legs in the air to the rhythm. At one point, his right sandal hit the taxi's plastic ashtray, knocking it onto the floor. Except for a chewing gum wrapper, it was empty, so no trash was spilled. I had already bent to pick it up when the driver suddenly braked, turned around, and with his face really close to my three-year-old son's, began screaming. "You stupid kid. You broke my car, you idiot!"

"Hey, are you crazy or something?" I shouted at the driver. "Yelling at a three-year-old because of a piece of plastic? Turn around and start driving or, I swear, next week you'll be shaving corpses in the Abu Kabir morgue, because you won't be driving any public vehicle, you hear me?" When I saw that he was about to say something, I added, "Shut your mouth now and drive."

The driver gave me a look that was full of hatred. The possibility of his smashing in my face and losing his job was in the air. He considered it for a long moment, took a deep breath, turned around, shifted into first gear, and drove.

On the taxi's radio, Bobby McFerrin was singing "Don't Worry, Be Happy," but I felt very far from happy. I looked at Lev. He wasn't crying, and even though we were stuck in a very slow-moving traffic jam, it wouldn't take long to reach my parents' house. I tried to find another ray of light in that unpleasant ride, but couldn't. I smiled at Lev and tousled his hair. He looked at me hard, but didn't smile back. "Daddy," he asked, "what did the man say?"

"The man said," I answered quickly, as if it were nothing, "that when you're riding in a car, you have to watch how you move your legs so you don't break anything."

Lev nodded, looked out the window, and a second later asked again, "And what did you say to the man?"

"Me?" I said to Lev, trying to gain a little time. "I told the man that he was absolutely right, but that he should say whatever he has to say quietly and politely, and not yell."

"But you yelled at him," Lev said, confused.

"I know," I said, "and that wasn't right. And you know what? I'm going to apologize now."

I leaned forward so that my mouth almost touched the thick, hairy neck of the driver and said loudly, almost declaiming, "Mr. Driver, I'm sorry I yelled at you, it wasn't right." When I finished, I looked at Lev and smiled again, or at least I tried. I looked out the window—we were just easing our way out of the traffic jam on Jabotinsky Street; the hard part was behind us.

"But Daddy," Lev said, putting his tiny hand on my knee, "now the man has to tell me he's sorry, too." I looked at the sweaty driver in front of us. It was clear to me that he was hearing our whole conversation. It was even clearer that asking him to apologize to a three-year-old was not a really good idea. The rope between us was stretched to the breaking point as it was. "Sweetie," I said, bending down to Lev, "you're a smart little boy and you already know lots of things about the world, but not everything. And one of the things you still don't know is that saying you're sorry might be the hardest thing of all. And that doing something so hard while you're driving could be very, very dangerous. Because while you're trying to say you're sorry, you can have an accident. But you know what? I don't think we have to ask the driver to say he's sorry because, just by looking at him, I can tell that he's sorry."

We'd already driven into Bialik Street—now there was only the right turn onto Nordau and then a left to Be'er Lane. In another minute, we'd be there. "Daddy," Lev said as he narrowed his eyes, "I can't tell that he's sorry." At that moment, in the middle of the incline on Nordau, the driver slammed on the brakes again and pulled up the hand brake. He turned around and moved his face close to my son's. He didn't say anything, just looked Lev in the eye, and a very long second later, whispered, "Believe me, kid, I'm sorry."

# My Lamented Sister

Nineteen years ago, in a small wedding hall in Bnei Brak, my older sister died, and she now lives in the most Orthodox neighborhood in Jerusalem. I recently spent a weekend at her house. It was my first Shabbat there. I often go to visit her in the middle of the week, but that month, with all the work I had and my trips abroad, it was either Saturday or nothing. "Take care of yourself," my wife said as I was leaving. "You're not in such great shape now, you know. Make sure they don't talk you into turning religious or something." I told her she had nothing to worry about. Me, when it comes to religion, I have no God. When I'm cool, I don't need anyone, and when I'm feeling shitty and this big empty hole opens up inside me, I just know there's never been a god that could fill it and there never will be. So even if a hundred rabbis pray for my lost soul, it won't do them any good. I have no God, but my sister does, and I love her, so I try to show him some respect.

The period when my sister was discovering religion was just about the most depressing time in the history of Israeli pop. The Lebanon War had just ended, and nobody was in the mood for upbeat tunes. But then again, all those ballads to handsome young soldiers who'd died in their prime were getting on our nerves, too. People wanted sad songs, but not the kind that carried on about some crummy unheroic war that everyone was trying to forget. Which is how a new genre came into being all of a sudden: the dirge for a friend who's gone religious. Those songs always described a close buddy or a beautiful, sexy girl who'd been the singer's reason for living, when out of the blue something terrible had happened and they'd turned Orthodox. The buddy was growing a beard and praying a lot; the beautiful girl was covered from head to toe and wouldn't do it with the morose singer anymore. Young people would listen to those songs and nod grimly. The Lebanon War had taken so many of their buddies that the last thing anyone wanted was to see the others just disappear forever into some yeshiva in the armpit of Jerusalem.

It wasn't only the music world that was discovering born-again Jews. They were hot stuff all over the media. Every talk show had a regular seat for a newly religious ex-celeb who made a point of telling everyone how he didn't miss his wanton ways in the least, or the former friend of a well-known born-again who'd reveal how much the friend had changed since turning religious and how you couldn't even talk to him anymore. Me, too. From the moment my sister crossed the lines in the direction of Divine Providence, I became a kind of local celebrity.

Neighbors who'd never given me the time of day would stop, just to offer me a firm handshake and pay their condolences. Hipster twelfth-graders, all dressed in black, would give me a friendly high five just before getting into the cab that would take them to some dance club in Tel Aviv. And then they'd roll down the window and shout to me how broken up they were about my sister. If the rabbis had taken someone ugly, they could've handled it; but grabbing someone with her looks—what a waste!

Meanwhile, my lamented sister was studying at some women's seminary in Jerusalem. She'd come visit us almost every week, and she seemed happy. If there was a week when she couldn't come, we'd go visit her. I was fifteen at the time, and I missed her terribly. When she'd been in the army, before going religious, serving as an artillery instructor in the south, I didn't see much of her, either, but somehow I missed her less back then.

Whenever we met, I'd study her closely, trying to figure out how she'd changed. Had they replaced the look in her eyes, her smile? We'd talk the way we always did. She still told me funny stories she'd made up specially for me, and helped me with my math homework. But my cousin Gili, who belonged to the youth section of the Movement Against Religious Coercion and knew a lot about rabbis and stuff, told me it was just a matter of time. They hadn't finished brainwashing her yet, but as soon as they did, she'd begin talking Yiddish, and they'd shave her head and she'd marry some sweaty, flabby, repulsive guy who'd forbid her to see me anymore. It could take another year or two, but I might as well brace myself, because once she was married, she might continue breathing, but from our point of view, it would be just as if she'd died.

Nineteen years ago, in a small wedding hall in Bnei Brak, my older sister died, and she now lives in the most Orthodox neighborhood in Jerusalem. She has a husband, a yeshiva student, just like Gili promised. He isn't sweaty or flabby or repulsive, and he actually seems pleased whenever my brother or I come to visit. Gili also promised me at the time, about twenty years ago, that my sister would have hordes of children and that every time I'd hear them speaking Yiddish like they were living in some godforsaken shtetl in eastern Europe, I'd feel like crying. On that subject, too, he was only half right, because she really does have lots of children, one cuter than another, but when they speak Yiddish it just makes me smile.

As I walked into my sister's house, less than an hour before Shabbat, the children greeted me in unison with their "What's my name?"—a tradition that began after I once got them mixed up. Considering that my sister has eleven, and that each of them has a double-barreled name, the way the Hasidim usually do, my mistake was certainly forgivable. The fact that all the boys are dressed the same way and decked out with identical sets of payos provides some pretty strong mitigating arguments. But all of them, from Shlomo-Nachman on down, still want to make sure that their peculiar uncle is focused enough, and gives the right present to the right nephew.

Once I'd passed the roll-call test with flying colors, I was treated to a strictly kosher glass of cola as my sister, who hadn't seen me in a long time, took her place on the other side of the living room and said she wanted to know what I'd been up to. She loves it when I tell her that I'm doing well and I'm happy, but since the world I live in is to her one of frivolities, she isn't really interested in the details. The fact that my sister will never read a single story of mine upsets me, I admit, but the fact that I don't observe the Sabbath or keep kosher upsets her even more.

I once wrote a children's book and dedicated it to my nephews. In the contract, the publishing house agreed that the illustrator would prepare one special copy in which all the men would have yarmulkes and payos, and the women's skirts and sleeves would be long enough to be considered modest. But in the end, even that version was rejected by my sister's rabbi, the one she consults on matters of religious convention. The children's story described a father who runs off with the circus. The rabbi must have considered this too reckless, and I had to take the "kosher" version of the book—the one the illustrator had worked on so skillfully for many hours—back to Tel Aviv.

Until about a decade ago, when I finally got married, the toughest part of our relationship was that my future wife couldn't come with me when I went to visit my sister. To be completely honest, I ought to mention that in the nine years we've been living together, we've gotten married dozens of times in all sorts of ceremonies that we made up ourselves: with a kiss on the nose at a fish restaurant in Jaffa, exchanging hugs in a dilapidated hotel in Warsaw, skinny-dipping on the beach in Haifa, or even sharing a Kinder egg on a train from Amsterdam to Berlin. Except that none of these ceremonies is recognized, unfortunately, by the rabbis or by the state. So that when I would go to visit my sister and her family, my girlfriend always had to wait for me at a nearby café or park. At first I was embarrassed to ask her to do that, but she understood the situation and accepted it. As for me, well, I accepted it as well—what choice did I have?—but I can't really say I understand.

Nineteen years ago, in a small wedding hall in Bnei Brak, my older sister died, and she now lives in the most Orthodox neighborhood in Jerusalem. Back then there was a girl that I loved to death but who didn't love me. I remember how two weeks after the wedding I went to visit my sister in Jerusalem. I wanted her to pray for that girl and me to be together. That's how desperate I was. My sister was quiet for a minute and then explained that she couldn't do it. Because if she prayed and then that girl and I got together and our togetherness turned out to be hell, she'd feel terrible. "I'll pray for you to meet someone you'll be happy with instead," she said, and gave me a smile that tried to be comforting. "I'll pray for you every day. I promise." I could see she wanted to give me a hug and was sorry she wasn't allowed to, or maybe I was just imagining it. Ten years later I met my wife, and being with her really did make me happy. Who said that prayers aren't answered?

# Bird's Eye

If not for my mother, there's a good chance we might have gone on thinking everything was fine.

It was an ordinary Saturday morning when she told us that her grandson had asked her to play a special game with him, a game you can only play on Mom's phone. It's really easy: all you have to do is shoot birds out of a slingshot so they can destroy buildings where green pigs live.

"Ah, Angry Birds," my wife and I said together, "our favorite game."

"I've never heard of it," my mother said.

"You are probably the only one," my wife said. "I think there are more Japanese soldiers hiding in the forests, not knowing that World War Two is over, than people on this planet who don't know this game. It is probably the most popular iPhone game ever."

"And I thought your favorite game was Go Fish with the cards of flowers of Israel," my mother said, offended.

"Not anymore," my wife said. "How many times can you ask someone without yawning whether they have a squill?"

"But that game," my mother said, "even though I watched it without my glasses, it looked like when those birds hit their targets, they die."

"They sacrifice themselves to achieve a greater goal," I said quickly. "It's a game that teaches values."

"Yes," my mother said. "But that goal is just to collapse buildings on the heads of those sweet little piglets that never did them any harm."

"They stole our eggs," my wife insisted.

"Yes," I said. "It's actually an educational game that teaches you not to steal."

"Or, more accurately," my mother said, "it teaches you to kill anyone who steals from you and to sacrifice your life doing it."

"They shouldn't have stolen those eggs," my wife said in the tear-choked voice that emerges when she knows she's about to lose an argument.

"I don't understand," my mother said. "Did those infant piglets themselves steal your eggs, or are we talking about collective punishment here?"

"Coffee, anyone?" I asked.

After coffee, our family broke its Angry Birds record when the teamwork between my son, an expert in shooting cluster birds that hit multiple targets, and my wife, an expert in launching birds with square-shaped iron heads that can penetrate anything, succeeded in collapsing an especially well fortified, beehive-shaped structure on the swollen green head of the mustached prince of pigs who said his last "Ho-la" and was then silenced forever.

While we ate cookies to celebrate our moral victory over the evil pigs, my mother started hassling us again. "What is it about that game that makes you love it so much?" she asked.

"I love the weird sounds the birds make when they crash into things," Lev said with a giggle.

"I love the physical-geometrical aspect of it," I said, shrugging. "That whole business of calculating angles."

"I love killing things," my wife whispered in a shaky voice. "Destroying buildings and killing things. It's so much fun."

"And it really improves coordination," I said, still trying to soften the effect. "Seeing those pigs exploding into pieces and their houses collapsing," my wife continued, her green eyes staring into infinity.

"More coffee, anyone?" I asked.

My wife was the only one in the family who really hit the nail on the head. Angry Birds is so popular in our home and in others because we truly love to kill and break things. So, it's true that the pigs stole our eggs in the short opener of the game, but between you and me, that's only an excuse for us to channel some good old rage in their direction. The more time I spend thinking about that game, the more clearly I understand something:

Under the adorable surface of the funny animals and their

sweet voices, Angry Birds is actually a game that is consistent with the spirit of religious fundamentalist terrorists.

I know it isn't really politically correct. But how else to explain a game in which you are prepared to sacrifice your life just so you can destroy the houses of unarmed enemies and vaporize their wives and children inside, causing their deaths? And that's before you get into the business of the pigs: a filthy animal that, in fanatic Muslim rhetoric, is often used to symbolize heretical races whose fate is death. After all, cows and sheep could just as easily have stolen our eggs, but the game planners still deliberately chose fat, dollar-green capitalist pigs.

By the way, I'm not saying that this is necessarily bad. I guess launching square-headed birds into stone walls is as close as I'll ever get to a suicide mission in this incarnation. So, this might be a fun, controlled way of learning that not only birds or terrorists get angry, but so do I, and all I need is the right and relatively harmless context in which to recognize that anger and let it run wild for a while.

A few days after that odd conversation with my mother, she and my father appeared at our door holding a rectangular gift wrapped in flowered paper. Lev opened it excitedly and found a board game inside, on which pictures of dollar bills were prominently featured.

"You said you were bored by Go Fish," my mother said, "so we decided to buy you Monopoly."

"What do you have to do in this game?" Lev asked suspiciously.

"Make money," my father said. "Lots of money! You take all

your parents' money till you're filthy rich and they're left with nothing."

"Great!" Lev said happily. "How do you play?"

And from that day on, the green pigs have been living in peace and quiet. True, we haven't been to their neighborhoods on Mom's iPhone, but I'm sure that if we dropped in for a quick visit, we'd find them squealing contentedly after closing off a balcony or digging a burrow for their little ones. My wife and I, on the other hand, find our situation deteriorating. Every evening, after Lev goes to sleep, we sit in the kitchen and calculate our new debts to our greedy little scion, who holds more than ninety percent of the Monopoly real estate, including cross-ownership of construction and infrastructure companies. After we finish calculating our multidigit debts, we go to bed. I close my eyes, trying not to think about the chubby, coldhearted issue of our loins who, in the near future, is going to strip my wife and me of the torn carton we're presently living in on the game board, till blessed sleep finally arrives, and with it, dreams. Once again I'm a bird, flying across the blue skies, cutting through the clouds in a breathtaking blissful arc, only to crush my square head in a delirium of vengeance on the heads of green, mustached, egg-eating pigs. Ho-la!

# Year Five

# Imaginary Homeland

When I was a kid, I used to try to imagine Poland. My mother, who grew up in Warsaw, told me quite a few stories about the city, about Jerusalem Boulevard (Aleje Jerozolimskie), where she was born and played as a little girl, and about the ghetto where she spent her childhood years trying to survive and where she lost her entire family. Apart from one blurred photograph in my older brother's history book that showed a tall, mustached man and a horse-drawn carriage in the background, I had no reality-based images of that distant country, but my need to imagine the place where my mother grew up and where my grandparents and uncle are buried was strong enough to keep me trying to create it in my mind. I pictured streets like the ones I saw in illustrations in Dickens novels. In my mind, the churches my mother told me about were right out of a musty old copy of *The Hunchback of Notre Dame*. I could imagine her walking down those cobblestone streets, careful not to bump into tall, mustached men, and all the images I invented were always in black-and-white.

My first encounter with the real Poland took place a decade ago, when I was invited to the Warsaw Book Fair. I remember feeling surprise when I walked out of the airport, a reaction I couldn't account for at the moment. Later, I realized that I had been surprised that the Warsaw spread before me was alive in Technicolor, that the roads were full of cheap Japanese cars, not horse-drawn carriages, and yes, also that most of the people I saw were utterly clean-shaven.

Over the past decade, I traveled to Poland almost every year. I kept getting invitations to visit, and although I had generally been cutting down on flying, I found it hard to refuse the Poles. Although most of my family had perished under horrendous circumstances there, Poland was also the place where they had lived and thrived for generations, and my attraction to that land and its people was almost mystic. I went looking for the house my mother was born in, and found a bank there. I went to another house where she had spent a year of her life and found that it was now a grassy field. Strangely enough, I didn't feel frustrated or sad, and even took pictures of both sites. True, I would rather have found a house instead of a bank or a field. But a bank, I thought, was better than nothing.

During my last visit to Poland a few weeks ago, for a book festival in another part of the country, a charming photographer named Elżbieta Lempp asked if she could take my picture. I agreed happily. She photographed me in a café, where I was waiting for my reading to take place, and on returning to Israel,

I found that she had e-mailed me a copy of the picture. It was a black-and-white shot of me talking to a tall, mustached man. Behind us, out of focus, was an old building. Everything in the photograph seemed to be taken not from reality, but from my childhood imaginings of Poland. Even the expression on my face looked Polish and frighteningly serious. I stared at the image. If I could have unfrozen my photographed self from his pose, he could have walked right out of the frame and actually found the house where my mother was born. If he were brave enough, he might even have knocked on the door. And who knows who would have opened it for him: the grandmother or grandfather I never knew, maybe even a smiling little girl who had no idea what the cruel future had in store for her. I stared at the picture for quite a while, until Lev came into the room and saw me sitting there, eyes glued to the computer screen. "How come that picture has no colors?" he asked. "It's magic," I said, and smiled and ruffled his hair.

# Fat Cats

In preparation for the meeting with Lev's preschool teacher, I shaved and took my good suit out of the closet.

"It's a ten-in-the-morning meeting," my wife said, laughing. "The teacher will probably be wearing sweatpants. And with that white shirt and jacket, you'll look like a groom."

"Like a lawyer," I corrected her. "And when the meeting's over, you'll thank me for dressing up."

"Why are you acting like she wants to talk to us because Lev did something bad?" my wife protested. "Maybe she just wants to tell us that Lev is a good kid who helps the other kids in his group?"

I tried to picture our Lev in the preschool yard generously sharing his sandwich with a scrawny, grateful classmate who forgot to bring a snack that day. The incredible strain from trying to conjure up that image almost gave me a stroke. "Do you really think they asked us to come in to hear about something nice Lev did?" I argued. "No," she admitted sadly. "I just like arguing with you."

The teacher was actually wearing sweatpants, but she really liked my suit and enjoyed hearing that it was the same suit I wore to my wedding.

"But back then he could still wear it without having to hold in his stomach," my wife said, and she and the teacher exchanged the empathetic smiles of women stuck with men who have three pizzerias on speed dial but have never seen the inside of a gym.

"Actually," the teacher said, "the reason I asked you to come in does have something to do with food."

The teacher told us that little Lev had forged a secret pact with the preschool cook, that she was bringing him chocolate on a regular basis, even though the board of education had strictly prohibited children from eating sweets on school grounds. "He goes to the bathroom and comes back with five chocolate bars," the teacher explained. "Yesterday, he sat in a corner and kept eating until streams of chocolate started running out of his nose."

"But why don't you talk to the cook about it?" my wife asked.

"I've already done that," the teacher sighed. "But she says Lev is so manipulative that she just can't help it."

"And you think it's possible," my wife continued, "that a five-year-old can control an adult and force her to—"

"Don't pay attention to her," I whispered to the teacher. "She knows it's possible. She just likes to argue."

In the afternoon, I took advantage of a friendly soccer game with Lev to have a heart-to-heart. "You know what Ricki the teacher told me today?" I asked.

"That even though I water her computer every morning, it doesn't help, and the screen will always stay a midget?" Lev asked.

"No," I said. "She told me that Mari the cook brings you chocolate every morning."

"Yes," Lev said happily. "Lots and lots and lots of chocolate."

"Ricki also said that you eat all the chocolate yourself and won't share it with the other kids," I added.

"Yes," Lev agreed quickly. "But I can't give them any because kids aren't allowed to eat sweets in school."

"Very good," I said. "But if kids aren't allowed to eat sweets in school, why do you think you can?"

"Because I'm not a kid." Lev smiled a pudgy, sneaky smile. "I'm a cat."

"You're what?"

*"Meow,"* Lev answered in a soft, purry voice. *"Meow, meow, meow."*

The next morning, I was drinking coffee in the kitchen and reading the papers. The coach of the Israeli national soccer team was caught by customs smuggling more than $25,000 worth of cigars into the country. A Knesset member from the Shas Party bought a restaurant and forced his parliamentary aide, paid out of the Knesset budget, to work there. Basketball coaches for Maccabi Tel Aviv, the country's star team, are facing charges of income tax evasion. Then, while I ate breakfast, I read a little about the trial of former prime minister Ehud Olmert, accused of graft, and topped it all off with a short item stating that former finance minister Avraham Hirschson, currently incarcerated for embezzlement, has been called "a model prisoner" by his fellow inmates.

For years I've struggled in vain to understand why such well-heeled, successful people choose to break the law, risking punishment and scorn, when they already have everything. Olmert, after all, was not living in abject poverty when he forged flight expenses so he could squeeze another thousand dollars out of Yad Vashem. And Hirschson wasn't exactly starving when he embezzled money from the organization for which he was working. But then, after that heart-to-heart with Lev, it all became clear. Those men, just like my son, cheat and steal and lie only because they are sure they are cats. And as adorable, furry, cream-loving creatures, they don't have to abide by the same rules and laws all those sweaty two-legged creatures around them have to obey. With that in mind, it's easy to predict the former prime minister's line of defense:

*Prosecutor:* Mr. Olmert, are you aware of the fact that forgery and fraud are against the law?

*Olmert:* Of course. As a moral, law-abiding former prime minister, I am completely aware that they are against the law for all the citizens of the country. But if you read the country's laws carefully, you will see that they don't apply to cats! And I, sir, have been well known throughout the world as a lazy fat cat.

**Prosecutor** (flabbergasted): Mr. Olmert, certainly you do not expect the court to take your last remark seriously.

**Olmert** (licking the cuffs of his Armani suit): *Meow, meow, meow.*

# Poser

The media-blitzed revolution in Libya isn't the only one going on in the region; another revolution, quiet but no less significant, is taking place. After more than forty years of being oppressed by substandard nutrition and deprived of physical activity, my body has taken to the streets. One after another, in remarkable synchronization, my muscles have begun to cramp. It started with my neck, moved down to my shoulders, and at some point even reached my feet. My wife came home one day to find me lying on my back like a dead cockroach. It took her twenty minutes to understand that something was wrong with me, and when she did, the first thing she said was, "You had it coming." The second thing she said had to do with a bet she'd made with my cousin from Ramat Gan that I would die of a heart attack before I reached fifty. According to my wife, the only reason he agreed to risk money on my longevity was his strong feelings for me; she had common sense and modern medicine on her side. "Anyone treating a pet the way you treat your body would have been sued by PETA a long time ago," my wife pointed out as she tried to help me sit up. "Why can't you be like me—watch what you eat, do yoga?"

The truth is, I did try yoga a few years ago. At the end of my first beginners' class, the pale, skinny teacher came over to me and in a soft but firm voice explained that I wasn't ready yet to work with the beginners and should first join a "special" group. The special group turned out to be a bunch of women in advanced stages of pregnancy. It was actually quite nice—the first time in a long while that I was the one with the smallest belly in the room. The women working out were very slow, and they would pant and sweat even when they were asked to perform simple, basic actions, just like me. I was sure that I had finally found my place in the cruel world of physical activity. But the group steadily grew smaller: as on a reality show, each week another woman was eliminated, and in trembling voices her excited friends would say that she had given birth.

About three months after I joined the class, all the members had given birth except me, and the teacher with the soft but firm voice told me before turning out the lights in the studio for the last time that she'd bought a one-way ticket to India and didn't know whether she'd come back. Meanwhile, she recommended that I take on something "a little less challenging than yoga." Since she didn't offer any details, I infused her enigmatic remark with the familiar aroma of basil and went back to eating whole trays of pizza.

So, when the recent wave of cramped muscles weakened a

little, I decided to be proactive and wrote down a list of potential physical activities, then crossed out all those I knew my body would not withstand. Running and working out in a gym were the first to go, joined by aerobics and spinning (given a choice between listening to Britney Spears and having a blocked aorta, I'd pick the latter), and kickboxing and Krav Maga (in the neighborhood of my youth, I'd been hit so many times for free that I couldn't imagine paying for the privilege). The only line that remained on the page after the series of crossings-out was fast walking. I quickly crossed out the word *fast* and added a question mark after *walking*.

Reading the page, my wife didn't seem excited about the walking-with-a-question-mark option. "There are a million other things that even someone as lazy and atrophied as you can do," she claimed.

"Name one," I said.

"Pilates," she said, munching on a wheat sprout or whatever that smelly thing in her hand was. A bit of quick research on Pilates turned up a few of its more attractive aspects: Even though it was officially defined as "physical activity," there was no danger you'd break a sweat while doing it, as most of the activity takes place while you're lying on your back. Also, the man who invented Pilates used the technique during World War I to rehabilitate wounded soldiers. Which meant that even if I didn't find a group of pregnant women to join, there was still a chance I might meet the criteria for being accepted into a class.

At my first lesson, I learned a few more facts about this

wonderful sport. In Pilates, you work on mainly internal muscles, which means that anyone watching you has no way of knowing whether you're really exercising your deep pelvic muscle, contracting your striated muscles, or just dozing on the mattress. Here in Israel, the classes are particularly small and made up mainly of injured ballet dancers. Which means that the studio abounds with such high levels of refinement, injuries, and empathy that there is no better place in the galaxy to complain about a pulled muscle and get a compassionate massage. I don't know when you last had five lame ballet dancers help you relax your hamstring, but if it's too long ago, I recommend heading straight for the nearest Pilates studio and trying it.

It's been only two weeks since I started doing Pilates. I still can't open pickle jars with my striated muscles and when I raise my hand to scratch my head the pain in my shoulder remains unbearable, but I do have my own locker, sweatpants with a gold stripe down each leg just like David Beckham, and a soft new mattress that I can lie down on twice a week for a whole hour and think about whatever I want as I stare at shapely, stoic-faced ballerinas perched on giant, brightly colored rubber balls.

# Just Another Sinner

A while ago, I took part in a group reading at an artists' colony in New Hampshire. Each of the three participants got to read for fifteen minutes. The other two were just starting out as writers and still hadn't published anything, so in a gesture of either generosity or condescension, I offered to read last. The first writer, a guy from Brooklyn, was pretty talented. He read something about his grandfather, who had died, strong stuff. The second writer, a woman from Los Angeles, began to read and sent my brain spinning. Sitting on my uncomfortable wooden chair in the overheated library auditorium of the artists' colony, I listened to my fears, my desires, the violence that smolders in me like an eternal flame but conceals itself so well that only it and I know it exists. In twenty minutes it was over. She left the podium for me, and as I walked limply past her, she gave me a pitying glance, the kind a proud lion in the jungle gives to a circus lion.

I don't remember exactly what I read that evening, only that throughout the reading, her story was reverberating through my mind. In that story, a father is speaking to his children, who are spending their summer vacation torturing animals. He tells them that there is a line that separates killing bugs from killing frogs, and that no matter how hard it is, that line must never be crossed.

Such is the way of the world. The writer didn't create it, but he's here to say what needs to be said. There is a line that separates killing bugs from killing frogs, and even if the writer has crossed it during his life, he still has to point it out. The writer is neither saint nor tzaddik nor prophet standing at the gate; he's just another sinner who has a somewhat sharper awareness and uses slightly more precise language to describe the inconceivable reality of our world. He doesn't invent a single feeling or thought—all of them existed long before him. He's not the least bit better than his readers—sometimes he's a lot worse—and so it should be. If the writer were an angel, the abyss that separates him from us would be so great that his writing couldn't get close enough to touch us. But because he's here, at our side, buried up to his neck in mud and filth, he's the one who, more than anyone else, can share with us everything that's going on in his mind, in the lit-up areas and especially in the dark recesses. He won't take us to the promised land, he won't bring peace to the world or heal the sick. But if he does his work right, a few more virtual frogs will get to live. The bugs, I'm sorry to say, will have to manage on their own.

From the day I began writing, I knew that truth. I knew it

firmly and clearly. But at that reading, when I came face-to-face with a real lion in the MacDowell Colony in the heart of New Hampshire and felt that fear for a second, I realized that even the sharpest knowledge we all possess can become blunted. Someone who creates without support or reinforcement, who can write only after working hours, surrounded by people who aren't even sure he has talent, will always remember that truth. The world around him just won't let him forget it. The only kind of writer who can forget is a successful one, the kind who doesn't write against the stream of his life, but with it, and every insight that flows from his pen not only enhances the text and makes him happy but also delights his agents and his publisher. Damn it, I forgot it. That is, I remembered that there's a line between one thing and another; it's just that lately it has some-how turned into a line between success and failure, acceptance and rejection, appreciation and scorn.

That night, after the reading, I went back to my room and straight to bed. Through the windows I could see huge pine trees and a clear night sky, and could hear frogs croaking in the woods. That was the first time since I'd come there that the frogs felt safe enough to croak. I closed my eyes and waited for sleep, for silence. But the croaking didn't stop. At two in the morning, I got out of bed, went to the computer, and started to write.

# Shit Happens

I wrote my first story twenty-six years ago in one of the most heavily guarded army bases in Israel. I was nineteen then, a terrible, depressed soldier who was counting the days to the end of his compulsory service. I wrote the story during an especially long shift in an isolated, windowless computer room deep in the bowels of the earth. I stood in the middle of that neon-lit freezing room and stared at the page of print. I couldn't explain to myself why I wrote it or exactly what purpose it was supposed to serve. The fact that I had typed all those made-up sentences was exciting, but also frightening. I felt as if I had to find someone to read the story right away, and even if he didn't like or understand it, he could calm me down and tell me that writing it was perfectly all right, and not just another step on my road to insanity.

The first potential reader didn't arrive until fourteen hours later. He was a pockmarked sergeant who was supposed to relieve me and take the next shift. In a voice trying to sound calm, I told him that I'd written a short story and wanted him to read it. He took off his sunglasses and said indifferently, "Fuck off."

I went a few floors up to ground level. The recently risen sun blinded me. It was six-thirty in the morning, and I desperately needed a reader. As I usually do when I have a problem, I headed for my big brother's house.

I buzzed the intercom at the entrance to the building and my brother's sleepy voice answered. "I wrote a story," I said. "I want you to read it. Can I come up?" There was a short silence, and then my brother said in an apologetic tone, "Not a good idea. You woke up my girlfriend, and she's pissed." After another moment of silence, he added, "Wait there for me. I'll get dressed and come down with the dog."

A few minutes later, he appeared with his small, washed-out-looking dog. It was happy to go out for a walk so early. My brother took the printed page from my hand and started to read as he walked. But the dog wanted to stay and do its business in a dirt patch by a tree near the building entrance. It tried to dig its little paws in the ground and resist, but my brother was too immersed in reading to notice, and a minute later, I found myself trying to catch up to him as he quickly walked down the street, dragging along the poor dog behind him.

Luckily for the dog, the story was very short, and when my brother stopped two blocks later, it could finally regain its balance and, going back to its original plan, do its business.

"This story is awesome," my brother said. "Mind-blowing. Do you have another copy?" I said I did. He gave me a big-brother-proud-of-his-little-brother smile, then bent down and used the printed page to scoop up the dog's shit and drop it in the trash can.

That was the moment I realized that I wanted to be a writer.

Unintentionally, my brother had told me something: The story I had written wasn't the creased, shit-smeared paper now sitting in the bottom of the trash can on the street. That page was just a pipeline through which I could transmit my feelings from my mind to his. I don't know how a wizard feels the first time he manages to cast a spell, but it's probably something similar to what I felt at that moment; I had discovered magic that I needed to help me survive the two long years until my discharge.

# Last Man Standing

It was less than a week after 9/11, and Kennedy Airport looked like the set for a grade-B action movie: jumpy security guards in uniform patrolled the terminal, clutching rifles and shouting nervously at the thousands of passengers gathering in huge lines. I was supposed to fly to Amsterdam that day to participate in a groovy, cool arts festival of the surrealistic kind that only a mellow Dutch hippie who spent the '60s tripping out could hallucinate.

After months as an artist in residence in the States, I was happy to get away. Amsterdam wasn't Israel, but it was still close enough for the love of my life to agree to fly there to be with me for a few days. And knowing that after the festival I'd be going back to America for two more tough months as a swarthy foreigner with an accent and a passport from the Middle East, I was in almost desperate need of that break.

Electronic tickets were less common back then, and the

friendly organizer had written to tell me that my ticket would be waiting at the KLM counter at the airport. The unpleasant woman at the counter insisted that there was no ticket waiting for me there. That shook me up a little. I called the festival organizer in Holland, who answered in a cheerful, but sleepy voice. After telling me how good it was to hear from me, he remembered that he'd forgotten to send the ticket. "What a bummer," he said. "My short-term memory isn't what it used to be." He suggested that I buy a ticket at the airport and when I landed, he'd reimburse me. When I told him that the ticket would probably be expensive, he said, "Man, don't even think about it. Buy the lousy ticket even if it costs a million. You have a cool event scheduled for tomorrow and we need you here."

The sour-faced lady demanded $2,400 for a middle seat in economy class, but I didn't even try to argue. A cool event and my beloved wife, who was my beloved girlfriend back then, were waiting for me in Amsterdam. I knew that I had to get on that plane. The flight was completely full, and the passengers looked a little nervous and tense. I knew this wasn't going to be an easy flight, but it became harder when I discovered that sitting in my seat, between a nun and a bespectacled Chinese man, was a bearded guy with tattooed arms, wearing sunglasses and looking like ZZ Top's fat, evil brother.

"Excuse me," I said to the beard somewhat timidly, "but you're sitting in my seat."

"It's my seat," the beard said. "Scram."

"But my boarding pass says that this is my seat," I persisted. "Look."

"I don't wanna look," the beard said, ignoring my out-stretched hand. "I told you, this is my seat. So scram."

At this point, I decided to call the flight attendant. She managed to get a little more cooperation out of the beard, and it turned out that, because of a computer error, we'd each gotten a boarding pass with the same seat number on it. In an authoritative voice, she said that since the flight was completely full, one of us would have to get off the plane.

"I say we should toss a coin," I told the beard. The truth is that I was desperate to stay on the plane, but that seemed like the only fair way to solve that exasperating problem. "No coins," the beard said, "I'm sitting in the seat. You're not. Get off the plane."

It was then that I felt one of the already overloaded circuits in my brain finally blow. "I am not getting off the plane," I told the flight attendant, who'd just come back to tell us that we were holding up a planeload of passengers. "I am asking you to get off now," she said in a cold voice, "or I'll be forced to call security."

"Call security," I said in a tearful voice, "call security to drag me off. It'll just add a few more zeroes to the amount I'll be suing your airlines for. I paid good money for a ticket. I received a boarding pass. I boarded the plane, and this is exactly where the story ends. If there aren't enough seats on the plane, you can get off yourself. I'll serve the food to the passengers."

The flight attendant didn't call security. Instead, the white-haired, blue-eyed pilot appeared, placed a soothing hand on my shoulder and asked me politely to get off the plane. "I am not getting off," I told him, "and if you try to take me off by force, I'll sue all of you. All of you, do you hear me? This is America, you know. People have been awarded millions for a lot less than this." And at that moment, which was supposed to be especially threatening, I began to cry.

"Why do you have to fly to Amsterdam?" he asked. "Is someone in your family ill?" I shook my head.

"So what is it, a girl?"

I nodded. "But it's not about her," I said. "It's just that I can't be here anymore." The pilot was silent for a moment, then asked, "Have you ever flown in a jump seat?" I managed to control my tears enough to say no.

"I'm warning you in advance," he said with a smile, "it's very uncomfortable. But it'll get you out of here, and you'll have a good story to tell." And he was right.

# Bemusement Park

When I was a little boy, my father took me to visit a family friend who was missing a finger. When he saw me staring at his four-fingered hand, the man told me he used to work in a factory. One day, his wristwatch fell into a machine, and when he instinctively reached into its guts, the sharp blades severed his finger.

"It was just a split second," he said with a sigh. "But by the time my brain told my arm it was better off not digging into that machine, I had nine fingers left."

I remember listening carefully and trying to look sad. But the powerful sense of hubris pulsing deep inside me told me that these sorts of things may happen to unlucky strangers, but not to me.

"If I ever drop a watch into a machine full of blades," I thought to myself, "there's no way I'll do something stupid like reach in to get it."

I thought about that story a few weeks ago, on the morning my wife and I told our son, Lev, who is almost six years old, that we were going on a family trip to Paris. My wife talked excitedly about the Eiffel Tower and the Louvre, and I mumbled something about the Pompidou Center and the Luxembourg Gardens. Lev just shrugged and asked wearily if we could go to Eilat instead. "It's just like going abroad," he reasoned, "except everyone speaks Hebrew."

And then it came, that split-second error that I would pay for dearly. The kind of mistake that leaves you with the right number of digits, admittedly, but inflicts an emotional scar from which you can never recover.

"Have you ever heard of Euro Disney?" I asked in a cheerful voice, bordering on hysteria.

"Euro-what?" asked Lev. "What's that?"

My wife immediately stepped in with her well-honed survival instincts. "Oh, nothing," she said. "It's just this place where— you know, it's really far away and very silly. Come on, let's look at some pictures of the Eiffel Tower on the Web."

But Lev had perked up now: "I don't want to see the Eiffel. I want to see pictures of the place Dad just said."

That afternoon, when the boy went to his capoeira class, where they've spent the past two years teaching him how to expertly kick his peers to a Brazilian beat, I approached my wife and asked for forgiveness: "He sounded so unexcited about the trip, and I just wanted to cheer him up."

"I know," she said, and hugged me warmly. "Don't worry.

Whatever it is we have to get through, it'll go by quickly. However horrible it is, it's just one little day in the rest of our lives."

Two weeks later, on a gray, damp Sunday morning, we found ourselves shivering in the square outside what's now called Disneyland Paris. Sad employees in happy uniforms physically blocked our access to the rides. "Entrance is currently permitted only to residents of the Disney Hotel and holders of the Disney Passport, which may be purchased at the box office," one of them explained in a throaty, doleful Amy Winehouse voice.

"I'm cold," Lev whimpered. "I want that lady to let us in."

"She can't," I said, and breathed some warm air on his nose in a pathetic attempt to melt the frozen snot hanging from his nostrils.

"But those kids went in," he wailed, pointing at a cheery group of children who waved their shiny Mickey Passports at Ms. Winehouse. "How come they get to go in and I don't?"

I tried an inappropriately serious response: "Remember how we talked about the social protest in summer? About how not everyone gets the same opportunities?"

"I want Mickey!" the boy whined. "I want to talk to Mickey about this. If he and Pluto knew what that lady was doing, they'd let us in."

"Mickey and Pluto don't really exist," I said. "And even if they did, how likely is it that a dog and a mouse could influence the profit-maximization policy of a successful publicly traded conglomerate? Chances are, if Mickey came to our aid, he'd be fired in—"

"Popcorn!" the boy yelled. "I want popcorn! Glow-in-the-dark popcorn like that fat girl is eating over there!"

After two boxes of unusually sticky popcorn that would become phosphorescent poop later that evening, Winehouse let us and another thousand or so desperate families in, and we all lunged at the rides. My peacenik wife, in her desire to avoid trampling a crying baby, briefly stepped aside, costing us another twenty minutes' wait for the Dumbo carousel. The line seemed very short when we were standing in it. That, perhaps, is the true genius of the place: the ability to snake the lines around in a way that always makes them look short. While we were waiting, I read a few interesting tidbits about Walt Disney on my iPhone. The site I was on claimed that, contrary to urban legend, Disney wasn't really a Nazi but just a regular anti-Semite who hated Communists and was overly fond of Germans.

Scattered around us in the confusing labyrinth of lines were some ornamental stone posts sprouting tiny plants. Lev complained that the miniature trees stank. At first I told him he was just imagining it, but after I saw the third father hold his son up above a post so he could pee on it, I realized that the same god who had blessed the park's designers with transcendental architectural wisdom had also blessed my son with keen senses. It was a little warmer by now, and Lev's snot was liquid again. My wife sent me off to find a tissue. On my quick excursion I discovered that anything you can buy with money could be easily obtained in the park, but unprofitable items such as bathrooms, straws, or napkins were virtually impossible to find. By the time

I got back to my family, Lev was gleefully climbing off the Dumbo carousel. He ran over and hugged me.

"Dad! That was fun!" As if on cue, a huge Mickey Mouse appeared and started chatting with the visitors.

"Tell Mickey," Lev instructed me, "that we want to open up a Shekel Disney just like this one in Israel."

"What's a Shekel Disney?" I asked.

"It's like here, but instead of taking euros from people, we'll take shekels," explained my financial midget.

Mickey came closer. Now he was within touching distance. I threw out a *"Bonjour"* in his direction, hoping to break the ice. "Welcome to Disneyland Paris!" Mickey replied, waving at us with a white-gloved, four-fingered hand.

# Year Six

# Ground Up

I have a good dad. I'm lucky, I know. Not everyone has a good dad. Last week, I went to the hospital with him for a fairly routine test, and the doctors told us that he was going to die. He has an advanced stage of cancer at the base of his tongue. The kind you don't recover from. Cancer had visited my father a couple of years earlier. The doctors were optimistic then and he really did beat it.

The doctors said there were several options this time. We could do nothing and my father would die in a few weeks. He could undergo chemotherapy, and if it worked it would give him another few months. They could give him radiation treatment, but chances were, that would hurt more than it would help. Or they could operate and remove his tongue and his larynx. It was a complicated surgery that would take more than ten hours, and, considering my father's advanced age, the doctors didn't think it was a viable option. But my dad liked the idea. "At my age, I don't need a tongue anymore, just eyes in my head and a heart that beats," he told the young oncologist. "The worst that can happen is that instead of telling you how pretty you are, I'll write it down."

The doctor blushed. "It's not just the speech, it's the trauma of the operation," she said. "It's the suffering and the rehabilitation if you survive it. We're talking here about an enormous blow to your quality of life."

"I love life." My dad gave her his obstinate smile. "If the quality is good, then great. If not, then not. I'm not picky."

In the taxi on our way back from the hospital my dad held my hand as if I were five years old again and we were about to cross a busy street. He was talking excitedly about the various treatment options, like an entrepreneur discussing new business opportunities. My dad is a businessman. Not a tycoon in a three-piece suit, just a regular guy who likes to buy and sell, and if he can't buy or sell, he's ready to lease or rent. For him, business is a way to meet people, to communicate, to get a little action going. Just let him buy a pack of cigarettes at some kiosk, and within ten minutes he's talking to the guy behind the counter about a possible partnership. "We're really in an ideal situation here," he said, totally seriously, as he stroked my hand. "I love making decisions when things are at rock bottom. And the situation is such dreck now that I can only come out ahead: With the chemo, I'll die in no time at all; with the radiation, I'll get gangrene of the jaw; and everyone's sure I won't survive the operation because I'm eighty-three. You know how many plots of land I bought like that? When the owner doesn't want to sell, and I don't have a penny in my pocket?"

"I know," I said. And I really do.

When I was seven, we moved. Our old apartment was on the same street, and we all loved it, but my dad insisted that we move to a larger place. During World War II, my dad, his parents, and some other people hid in a hole in the ground in a Polish town for almost six hundred days. The hole was so small that they couldn't stand or lie down in it, only sit. When the Russians liberated the area, they had to carry my father and my grandparents out, because they couldn't move on their own. Their muscles had atrophied. That time he spent in the hole had made him sensitive about privacy. The fact that my brother, sister, and I were growing up in the same room drove him crazy. He wanted us to move to an apartment where we would all have our own rooms. We kids actually liked sharing a bedroom, but when my dad makes up his mind, there's no changing it.

One Saturday a few weeks before we were supposed to leave our old apartment, which he'd already sold, my dad took us to see our new place. We all showered and put on our nicest clothes, even though we knew we weren't going to see anyone there. Still, it isn't every day you go to see your new apartment.

Though the building was finished, no one lived in it yet. After making sure we were all in the elevator, Dad pressed the button for the fifth floor. It was one of the few buildings in the neighborhood that had an elevator, and even the short ride was thrilling. Dad opened the reinforced-steel door to the new apartment and began to show us the rooms. First the kids' rooms, then the master bedroom, and finally the living room and the huge balcony. The view was amazing and all of us, especially my dad, were enchanted by the magical palace that would be our new home.

"Have you ever seen such a view?" he said, hugging my mom and pointing to the green hill visible from the living room window.

"No," my mom replied unenthusiastically.

"Then why the sour look?" my dad asked.

"Because there's no floor," my mom whispered, and looked down at the dirt and exposed metal pipes under our feet. Only then did I look down and see, along with my brother and sister, what my mother saw. I mean, we'd all seen earlier that there was no floor, but somehow, with all my dad's excitement and enthusiasm, we hadn't paid much attention to that fact. My dad looked down now, too.

"Sorry," he said. "There was no money left."

"After we move, I'll have to wash the floor," my mom said in her most ordinary voice. "I know how to wash tiles, not sand."

"You're right," my dad said, and tried to hug her.

"The fact that I'm right won't help me clean the house," she said.

"OK, OK," my dad said. "If you stop talking about it and

give me a minute's quiet, I'll think of something. You know that, right?"

My mother nodded unconvincingly. The elevator ride down was less happy.

When we moved into the new apartment a few weeks later, the floors were completely covered in ceramic tiles, a different color in each room. In the socialist Israel of the early 1970s, there was only one kind of tile—the color of sesame—and the colored floors in our apartment—reds, blacks, and browns—were different from anything we'd ever seen.

"You see?" My dad kissed my mother on the forehead proudly. "I told you I'd think of something."

Only a month later did we discover exactly what he'd thought of. I was alone at home taking a shower that day when a gray-haired man wearing a white button-down shirt came into the bathroom with a young couple. "These are our Volcano Red tiles. Direct from Italy," he said, pointing to the floor. The woman was the first to notice me, naked and soaped up, staring at them. The three of them quickly apologized and left the bathroom.

That evening at dinner, when I told everyone what had happened, my dad revealed his secret. Since he hadn't had the money to pay for floor tiles, he'd made a deal with the ceramics company: they would give us the tiles for free, and my dad would let them use our place as a model apartment.

The taxi had already reached my parents' building, and when we got out, my dad was still holding my hand. "This is exactly how I like to make decisions, when there's nothing to lose and everything to gain," he repeated. When we opened the apartment door, we were greeted by a pleasant, familiar smell; hundreds of colored floor tiles; and a single powerful hope. Who knows? Maybe this time, too, life and my father will surprise us with another unexpected deal.

# Sleepover

Here's an interesting fact about my screwed-up personality that I've learned over the years: When it comes to taking on a commitment, there's an inverse correlation between the proximity of the request in terms of time and my willingness to commit to it. So, for example, I might politely refuse my wife's modest request to make her a cup of tea today, but I will generously agree to go grocery shopping tomorrow. I have no problem saying that I will volunteer, in a month's time, to help some distant relative move to a new apartment; and if we're talking about six months from now, I'd even offer to wrestle a polar bear naked. The only significant problem with this character trait is that time keeps moving forward and in the end, when you find yourself shaking with cold on some frozen Arctic tundra facing a white-furred bear with bared teeth, you can't help asking yourself if it might not have been better to just say no half a year earlier.

On my last trip to Zagreb, Croatia, to participate in a writers' festival, I didn't find myself wrestling with any polar bears, but I got close enough. On the way to the hotel, while I was going over the schedule of events with Roman, the organizer of the festival, he nonchalantly tossed the following comment my way: "And I hope you didn't forget that you agreed to take part in a cultural project of ours and spend tonight in a local museum." In fact, I'd completely forgotten, or more precisely, I'd totally repressed the recollection. But later, at the hotel, I saw that I'd received an e-mail seven months earlier asking if, during the festival, I'd be willing to spend a night in the Zagreb Museum of Contemporary Art and then write about the experience. My reply consisted of two words: Why not?

But now, sitting in my pleasant, comfortable hotel room, picturing myself in a locked, dark museum, sprawled on a rusty, bumpy metal sculpture called something like *Yugoslavia, a Country Divided*, and covered by a tattered curtain I'd pulled off the entrance to the coatroom, the opposite question came to mind: Why yes?

After the literary event, I'm sitting with the other participants around a wooden table in a local bar. It's almost midnight when Carla, Roman's assistant, says that it's time to say good night to everyone. I need to go to the museum. The writers, some slightly drunk, get up and bid me a rather dramatic farewell. The brawny Basque poet hugs me tightly and says, "Hope to see you tomorrow"; a German translator wipes away a tear after shaking my hand, or maybe she was readjusting a contact lens.

The night guard at the museum doesn't know a word of English, let alone Hebrew. He leads me through a series of dark halls to a side elevator that takes us up one floor to a beautiful, spacious room with a neatly made bed in the middle. He makes a gesture that I take to mean I should feel free to wander around the museum. I thank him with a nod.

As soon as the guard leaves, I get into bed and try to go to sleep. I still haven't recovered from the early-morning flight, and the beers after the event haven't done much to keep me alert. My eyes begin to close, but another part of my brain refuses to submit. How many times in my life will I have the opportunity to wander around an empty museum? It would be a waste not to take a short stroll. I get up, put on my shoes, and take the elevator downstairs. The museum isn't huge, but in the near darkness, it's hard to find my way around. I walk past paintings and sculptures and try to remember them so that I can use them as landmarks to find my way to the elevator that will take me back to my comfortable bed. In a few minutes, the fear and tiredness fade a little, and I'm able to see the exhibited work not only as landmarks but also as pieces of art. I find myself walking circles through the halls. I always return to the same place. I sit down on the floor in front of a huge photograph of a gorgeous girl whose eyes seem to bore right into me. The text scrawled across the photo quotes graffiti sprayed on by an unknown Dutch soldier who was part of the UN Protection Force sent to Bosnia in 1994:

### No Teeth . . . ?
### A Mustache . . . ? Smel Like Shit . . . ?
### Bosnian Girl!

The powerful work reminds me of something I heard that afternoon in Zagreb in a side-street café. A waiter there told me that during the war, people who came in had a hard time choosing the right word when they wanted to order coffee. The word *coffee*, he explained, is different in Croatian, Bosnian, and Serbian, and every innocent word choice was fraught with threatening political connotations. "To avoid trouble," he'd said, "people started ordering espresso, which is a neutral Italian word, and overnight, we stopped serving coffee here and served only espresso."

As I sit in front of the painting and think about words, about xenophobia and hatred in the place I come from and the place I'm in now, I notice the sun is beginning to rise. The night is over, and I never got to enjoy the luxury of the soft bed the guard had made up for me.

I get up from where I've been sitting in a corner of the room and say good-bye to the beautiful girl in the picture. In daylight, she's even more beautiful. It's already eight a.m.; I start walking toward the exit as the first visitors, city guides in hand, make their way in.

# Boys Don't Cry

My son, Lev, complains that he has never seen me cry. He's seen his mother cry several times, especially when she reads him a story with a sad ending. He once saw his grandmother cry, on his third birthday, when he told her that his wish was that grandfather would get well. He even saw his kindergarten teacher cry when she received a phone call telling her that her grandfather had died. I was the only one he's never seen cry. And that whole business makes me uncomfortable.

There are many things parents are supposed to know how to do which I'm not very good at. Lev's kindergarten is full of fathers quick to pull their toolboxes out of their car trunks every time something breaks, and fix swings and water pipes without even working up a sweat. My son's father is the only one who never pulls a toolbox out of his car trunk, because he doesn't own a toolbox or a car. And even if he did, he wouldn't know how to fix anything. You'd expect a father like that—non-technical, an artist—to at least know how to cry.

133

"I'm not mad at you for not crying," Lev says, putting his little hand on my arm, as if he feels my discomfort, "I'm just trying to understand why. Why Mom cries and you don't."

I tell Lev that when I was his age, everything made me cry: movies, stories, even life. Every street beggar, run-over cat, and worn-out slipper made me burst into tears. The people around me thought that was a problem, and for my birthday they brought me a children's book meant to teach kids how not to cry. The book's protagonist cried a lot, till he met an imaginary friend who suggested that every time he felt the tears welling up, he should use them as fuel for something else: singing a song, kicking a ball, doing a little dance. I read that book maybe fifty times, and I practiced doing what it said over and over, till I was finally so good at not crying that it happened by itself. And now I'm so used to it, I don't know how to stop.

"So, when you were a kid," Lev asks, "every time you wanted to cry, you sang instead?"

"No," I admit reluctantly, "I don't know how to sing. So most of the time when I felt the tears coming, I hit someone instead."

"That's weird," Lev says in a contemplative voice, "I usually hit someone when I'm happy."

This feels like the right moment to go to the fridge and get us both some cheese sticks. We sit in the living room, nibbling quietly. Father and son. Two males. If you were to knock on the door and ask nicely, we'd offer you a cheese stick, but if you did something else instead, something that made us sad or happy, there's a good chance that you'd get roughed up a little.

# Accident

"Thirty years I'm a cabbie," the small guy sitting behind the wheel tells me, "thirty years and not one accident." It's been almost an hour since I got into his taxi in Beersheba and he hasn't stopped talking for a second. Under different circumstances I would tell him to shut up, but I don't have the energy for that today. Under different circumstances I wouldn't shell out 350 shekels to take a taxi to Tel Aviv. I would take the train. But today I feel that I have to get home as early as I can. Like a melting Popsicle that has to get back to the freezer, like a cell phone that urgently needs to be charged.

I spent last night at Ichilov Hospital with my wife. She had a miscarriage and was bleeding heavily. We thought it would be okay, till she passed out. It wasn't until we got to the emergency room that they told us that her life was in danger and gave her a blood transfusion, which was a perfect ending to a week in which my dad's doctors told me and my parents that the cancer at the base of his tongue was back.

The taxi driver repeats for the hundredth time that in thirty years he hasn't had a single accident and that, all of a sudden, five days ago, his car "kissed" the bumper of the car in front of him traveling at thirty miles per hour. When they stopped and checked, he saw that, except for a scratch on the left side of the bumper, the other car hadn't really been damaged at all. He offered the other driver two hundred shekels on the spot, but the driver insisted that they exchange insurance information. The next day, the driver, a Russian, asked him to come to a garage, and he and the owner—probably a friend of his—showed him a huge dent all the way on the other side of the car and said the damage was two thousand shekels. The cabdriver refused to pay, and now the other guy's insurance company was suing him.

"Don't worry, it'll be okay," I tell him, in the hope that my words will make him stop talking for a minute.

"How will it be okay?" he complains. "They're going to screw me. Those bastards are going to squeeze the money out of me. You see how unfair it is? Five days I haven't slept. Do you get what I'm saying?"

"Stop thinking about it," I suggest. "Try thinking about other things in your life. Happy things."

"I can't"—the cabdriver groans and grimaces—"I just can't."

"Then stop talking to me about it," I say. "Keep on thinking and suffering but just don't tell me about it anymore, OK?"

"It's not the money," the taxi driver continues, "believe me. It's the injustice that gets me."

"Shut up," I say, finally losing it, "just shut up for a minute."

"What are you yelling for?" the cabdriver asks, insulted. "I'm an old man. It's not nice."

"I'm yelling because my father is going to die if they don't cut his tongue out of his mouth," I continue to yell, "I'm yelling because my wife is in the hospital after a miscarriage." The driver is silent for the first time since I got into his taxi, and now I'm suddenly the one who can't stop the stream of words.

"Let's make a deal," I say. "Get me to an ATM and I'll take out two thousand shekels and give it to you. In exchange, it'll be your father who has to have his tongue removed and your wife who's lying in a hospital bed getting a blood transfusion after a miscarriage." The driver is still silent. And now, so am I. I feel a little uncomfortable for having shouted at him but not uncomfortable enough to apologize. To avoid his eyes, I look out the window. The road sign we pass says "Rosh Ha'ayin," and I realize that we missed the exit to Tel Aviv. I tell him that politely, or I shout it angrily, I don't recall anymore. He tells me not to worry. He doesn't really know the way, but in a minute, he'll find out.

A few seconds later he parks in the right lane of the highway, hoping to persuade another driver to stop. He starts to get out of the taxi to ask for directions to Tel Aviv. "You'll kill us both," I tell him. "You can't stop here."

"Thirty years I'm a cabbie," he tosses back at me as he gets out of the taxi, "thirty years and not one accident." Alone in the cab, I can feel the tears rising. I don't want to cry. I don't want to feel sorry for myself. I want to be positive, like my dad. My wife is fine now and we already have a wonderful son. My dad survived the Holocaust and has reached the age of eighty-three. That's not just a half-full glass; it's an overflowing one. I don't want to cry. Not in this taxi. The tears are welling up and will soon begin to flow. Suddenly I hear a crashing boom and the sound of windows breaking. The world around me shatters. A silver car veers across the next lane, completely smashed. The taxi moves, too. But not on the ground. It floats above it toward the concrete wall on the side of the road. After it hits, there's another bang. Another car must have hit the taxi.

In the ambulance, the paramedic wearing a yarmulke tells me I was very lucky. An accident like that with no deaths is a miracle. "The minute you're discharged from the hospital," he says, "you should run to the nearest synagogue and give thanks for still being alive." My cell phone rings. It's my dad. He's only calling to ask how my day at the university was and whether the little one is asleep yet. I tell him that the little one is sleeping and my day at the university was great. And that Shira, my wife, is fine too. She just stepped into the shower. "What's that noise?" he asks.

"An ambulance siren," I tell him. "One just passed by in the street."

Once, five years ago, when I was in Sicily with my wife and baby son, I called my dad to ask how he was. He said everything was fine. In the background, a voice on a loudspeaker was calling Dr. Shalman to the operating room. "Where are you?" I asked.

"In the supermarket," my dad said without a moment's hesitation. "They're announcing on the loudspeaker that someone lost her purse."

He sounded so convincing when he said that. So confident and happy.

"Why are you crying?" my dad asks now, from the other end of the line. "It's nothing," I say as the ambulance stops next to the emergency ward and the paramedic slams the ambulance doors open. "Really, it's nothing."

# A Mustache for My Son

**B**efore Lev's sixth birthday, we asked him if he'd like us to do anything special. He gave me and my wife a slightly suspicious look and asked why we had to do something special. I told him that we didn't have to, but that people usually do special things on their birthdays because it's a special day. If there was something Lev would like, I explained, like decorating the house, baking a cake, or taking a trip somewhere we don't usually go, his mother and I would be glad to oblige. And if not, we could just spend the day as usual. It was up to him. Lev stared at me intently for a few seconds and said, "I want you to do something special with your face."

And that's how the mustache was born.

The mustache is a hairy and mysterious creature, far more enigmatic than its woollier sibling, the beard, which clearly connotes distress (mourning, finding religion, being marooned on a desert island). The associations aroused by a mustache are more along the lines of *Shaft*, Burt Reynolds, German porn stars, Omar Sharif, and Bashar al-Assad—in short, the '70s and Arabs. So rather than "What's going on?" "How's the family?" or "Are you working on anything new?" it's only natural for an old acquaintance encountering your mustache for the first time to ask, "What's with the mustache?"

The timing of my new mustache—ten days after my wife miscarried, a week after I injured my back in a car crash, and two weeks after my father found out he had inoperable cancer—couldn't have been better. Instead of talking about Dad's chemo or my wife's hospitalization, I could divert all small talk to the thick tuft of facial hair growing above my upper lip. And whenever anyone asked, "What's with the mustache?" I had the perfect answer, and it was even mostly true: "It's for the boy."

A mustache is not just a great distraction device; it's also an excellent icebreaker. It's amazing how many people who see a new mustache in the middle of a familiar face are happy to share their own private mustache stories. That's how I found out that the acupuncturist who treats my newly aching back had been an officer in an elite Israel Defense Forces unit, and that he once had to draw a mustache on his face. "It sounds like a joke," he said, "but we went on an undercover operation once, disguised as Arabs, and they told us the two most important things were the mustache and the shoes. If you have a respectable mustache and believable shoes, people will take you for an Arab even if your parents are from Poland."

He remembered the operation well. It was in Lebanon, it was winter, and they were moving through open fields. They noticed a man wearing a kaffiyeh at some distance coming toward them. He had a weapon slung over his shoulder. They lay on the ground. Their orders were clear: If they encountered someone with a Kalashnikov, it was a terrorist and they had to shoot immediately; if he had a hunting rifle, it was probably just a shepherd.

My acupuncturist heard the two snipers in his unit arguing over the walkie-talkie. One of them claimed he could tell by the butt that it was a Chinese-made Kalashnikov. The other said it was too long to be a Kalashnikov—he thought it was an old rifle, and not an automatic. The man was getting closer. The first sniper kept asking for permission to open fire. The other sniper said nothing. My acupuncturist lay there in a sweat, a twenty-year-old boy with binoculars and a painted-on mustache, not knowing what to do. His first lieutenant whispered in his ear that if it really was a terrorist, they had to shoot before he spotted them.

Right at that moment, the man who had been walking toward them stopped, turned around, and took a whiz. My acupuncturist could now easily see through his binoculars that the man was carrying a large umbrella.

"That's it," said the acupuncturist as he pulled the last needle out of my left shoulder. "You can get dressed now." When I finished buttoning up my shirt and looked in the mirror, the mustache in the reflection looked completely unreal, exactly like the story I had just heard. The story of a kid with a scribble that looked like a mustache, who almost killed a man with an umbrella that looked like a rifle, on a covert operation that looked like a war. A day after Lev's birthday I'll shave this mustache off, after all. Reality here is confusing enough as it is.

# Love at First Whiskey

Five years ago my parents celebrated their forty-ninth anniversary under slightly painful conditions, my father sitting at the festive table with swollen cheeks and the guilty look of someone who's hidden nuts in his mouth. "Ever since his dental implant operation he looks like a scheming squirrel," my mother said with more than a little malice. "But the doctor promised that it'll pass in a week."

"She allows herself to talk like that," my father said in rebuke, "because she knows I can't bite her now. But don't worry, Mamele. We squirrels have long memories." And to prove that claim, my father went back fifty years to tell my wife and me how he and my mother first met.

My father was twenty-nine then and worked installing electrical infrastructures in buildings. Every time he finished a project, he'd go out and spend his wages carousing for two weeks, after which he'd stay in bed for two days to recuperate, and then go to work on a new project. On one of his sprees, he went to a Romanian restaurant on the Tel Aviv beach with a few friends. The food wasn't great, but the liquor was nice and the Gypsy troupe that played was fantastic. My father stayed to listen to the musicians and their plaintive melodies long after his friends had collapsed and were taken home. Even after the last of the diners had gone and the elderly owner insisted on closing, my father refused to part from the troupe, and with the help of a few compliments and some money, he managed to persuade the Gypsies to become his personal orchestra for the night. They walked down the beach promenade with him, playing magnificently. At one point, my drunk father had the uncontrollable urge to urinate, so he asked his private group to play a snappy tune suitable for such osmotic events. He then proceeded to a nearby wall to do what people do after excessive drinking. "Everything was just perfect," he said, smiling between his squirrel cheeks, "the music, the scenery, the light sea breeze."

A few minutes later, the euphoria was interrupted by a police car that had been called to arrest my father for disturbing the peace and demonstrating without a permit. It turned out that the wall he'd chosen to urinate on was the western wall of the French embassy, and the security guards thought that the man urinating to the accompaniment of a cheery band of Gypsy musicians was staging a creative political protest. They lost no time in calling the police. The policemen pushed my father, who was cooperating happily, into the backseat of the car. The seat was soft and comfortable, and after a long night my father was glad for a chance to take a little snooze. Unlike my father, the Gypsies were sober and resisted arrest, protesting vehemently that they hadn't done anything illegal. The police tried to shove them into the car, and in the struggle one musician's pet monkey bit the officer in charge. He responded with a loud yell that woke my father who, like any curious person, got right out of the car to find out what was going on. Outside the car he saw policemen and Gypsies fighting in a slightly comic battle, and behind them a few curious passersby who had stopped to watch the unusual show. Among them stood a beautiful redhead. Even through the alcohol haze, my father could tell that she was the most gorgeous woman he'd ever seen. He took his electrician's pad out of his pocket, grabbed the pencil he kept behind his right ear, always ready for action, went over to my mother, introduced himself as Inspector Ephraim Keret, and asked if she had been a witness to the incident. Frightened, my mother said she'd only just gotten there, but Dad insisted that he had to take her details so that he could question her later. She gave him her address, and before Inspector Ephraim could say anything else, two furious policemen jumped him, cuffed him, and dragged him to the car. "We'll be in touch," he yelled to Mom from the moving car with characteristic optimism. Mom went home quaking in fear and told her flatmate that a serial killer had cunningly managed to wheedle her address out of her. The next day, Dad arrived at my mother's doorstep, sober and carrying a bouquet of flowers. She refused to open the door. A week later, they went to a movie, and a year after that they were married.

Fifty years have passed. Inspector Ephraim Keret isn't in the electricity business anymore and my mother hasn't had a flatmate for a long time. But on special occasions like anniversaries, my father still pulls a special bottle of whiskey out of the cabinet, the same whiskey they served in the long-defunct Romanian restaurant, and pours everyone a shot. "When the doctor said only liquids for the first week, she meant soup, not that," Mom whispers to me as we all clink glasses. "Watch out, Mamele, I hear everything," Dad says, filling the space between his swollen cheeks with a sip of whiskey. "And in another ten days, I'll be allowed to bite again."

In the taxi on the way home from my parents' house, my wife says there's something about the story of how couples meet that hints at how they're going to live their lives together. "Your parents," she says, "met under colorful, extreme circumstances, and their life together continued to seem like a carnival."

"What about us?" I ask. I fell in love with my wife in a nightclub. She came in as I was about to leave. We'd known each other only very superficially before then. "I was just leaving," I shouted, trying to be heard over the noise of the music when we bumped into each other near the door. "I have to get up early tomorrow."

"Kiss me," she shouted back at me. I froze. From the little I knew about her, she had always seemed very shy, and that request was totally unexpected.

"Maybe I'll stay a little longer," I said.

A week later, we were a couple. A month later, I told her that her "Kiss me" at the nightclub door was the most daring thing I'd ever heard a girl say. She looked at me and smiled. "What I said was that you'd never find a taxi," she said. It is a good thing I misheard her.

"Us?" My wife thought for a moment in the taxi. "We're also like the way we met. Our life is one thing, and you always reinvent it to be something else more interesting. That's what writers do, right?"

I shrugged, feeling slightly rebuked. "Not that I'm complaining," my wife said, kissing me. "Compared to your family tradition of drunken peeing on embassy walls, you could say I got off cheap."

# Year Seven

# Shiva

One morning, my grandmother's brother decided to stop being religious. He shaved his beard, cut off his payos, shed his yarmulke, packed his things, and resolved to leave his hometown of Baranovichi and begin a new life. The town rabbi, considered a Talmudic prodigy, asked to see him before he left. The meeting between Avraham, my grandmother's brother, and the rabbi was brief and not very pleasant. The rabbi knew Avraham to be a gifted Torah student and was profoundly disappointed that he had decided to abandon religion. But he didn't mention that to Avraham; he merely gave him a piercing look and promised that he would not die before he returned to the ways of the Torah. It wasn't clear at the time if that was a blessing or a threat, but the words were spoken with such conviction that Avraham never forgot them.

I hear that story during the shiva for my father. My older brother is sitting to my right, and my sister is seated on a low stool to my left. I offered her my comfortable chair, but she said no. According to the customs of Jewish mourning, which my ultra-Orthodox sister strictly observes, the family of the deceased must sit on chairs lower than those of the people who have come to pay their condolences. Sitting across from us is a distant relative from the ultra-Orthodox city of Bnei Brak, and like many others who come to visit us during the shiva, he offers not only a bit of solace but also a new, totally unknown story about our father. It's amazing how many more sides there were to that man than the ones I knew when he was alive. And it's no less amazing that it's the total strangers, people I've never met before, who help me grow even closer to my father even now that he's gone.

The ultra-Orthodox relative from Bnei Brak doesn't eat or drink anything in our house during the shiva, refusing even a glass of water. I don't ask why, but it's quite clear that he doesn't completely trust us on matters of kashruth. All he does is tell the story. As if he's come here as a messenger, to place another story about Dad at our doorstep, offer a few restrained words of comfort, and leave. But before he goes, he has to finish the tale.

So where were we? That meeting between Avraham and the rabbi. Years after Avraham, Grandma's brother, left the yeshiva in Poland, immigrated to Israel, and joined a kibbutz, he found himself in the very heart of a terrible war. It was 1973, and on Yom Kippur, a surprise attack was launched against Israel. The Israeli army was caught unprepared, and during the first days of the war, everyone felt that the end of the State of Israel and of the Jewish people was approaching. Avraham was in a place that was being heavily bombarded by the Syrians, and with shells bursting everywhere around him, he stood up and called to a woman who was lying on the ground not far away to come and lie down beside him. The woman hurried over, and when she asked the supremely confident Avraham why he thought it was safer where he was, he explained that she should stay close to him because no shell would fall anywhere near him. "A lot of unlucky people are going to die in this damn war," Avraham said, trying to calm the frightened woman, "but I won't be one of them." Shouting over the whistling of the artillery shells, she asked how he could be so sure of that, and Avraham answered without hesitation, "Because I still haven't returned to the ways of the Torah." Avraham and the woman survived the bombing, and years later, when he fell into the sea during a storm, the rescue team found him thrashing in the water and shouting to the heavens, "I still don't believe in you!"

Avraham raised a large, thriving family and reached a ripe old age in relatively good health until serious illness struck. At one point, after he had lost consciousness, the doctors told his family that he would not last more than a day or so. But that day went on and on, and a few weeks later, when my dad visited Avraham's family and heard how much he was suffering, he asked them for a prayer book and a yarmulke, went straight to the hospital, entered Avraham's room, and prayed all night beside his bed. At dawn, Avraham died.

"It's not so hard to pray for the soul of a Jew when you're a believer," that relative says as he makes his way to the door. "As a religious man, I can tell you that it's very easy, like a reflex, almost involuntary. But for a secular man like your father to do it—he really has to be a tzaddik."

That night, when the last of the visitors has gone and our mother goes to bed, only my sister, my brother, and I are left in the living room. My brother is smoking a cigarette, staring out the window, and my sister is still seated on her low stool. Soon we'll all go to sleep in our childhood rooms. My parents left the three rooms exactly as they had been, as if they knew we'd come back one day. On the wall of my room is a poster of a comic book hero I loved as a child; in my brother's room, there's a map of the world hanging above his bed; and on the wall in my sister's room is a tapestry she embroidered when she was a teenager, depicting—of course—Jacob wrestling with a white-robed angel. But before we go to bed, we try to steal another few minutes alone together. The shiva ends tomorrow. My sister will go back to the ultra-Orthodox Jerusalem neighborhood of Mea Shearim and my brother will fly back to Thailand, but until then we can still have a cup of tea together, eat the strictly kosher cookies I brought for my sister from a special store, savor the stories we heard about our father during the week of mourning, and be proud of our dad without apology or criticism, just like children should.

# In My Father's Footsteps

It was the night I was supposed to fly from Israel to Los Angeles to kick off my book-promotion tour, and I didn't want to go.

My father had died only four weeks earlier, and this trip meant that I would miss the unveiling of his headstone. But my mother insisted. "Your father would want you to do it." And that was a very persuasive argument. My dad really would have wanted me to take that trip. When he first took sick, I had canceled all my travel plans, and even though he realized how important it was to both of us to be together during those difficult days, the cancellations still bothered him.

Now I was thinking about him and the book tour while I was giving Lev his bath. On the one hand, I thought, the last thing I wanted now was to get on a plane. On the other, maybe it would be good for me to be busy, to think about other things for a while. Lev sensed that my mind was somewhere else, and when I took him out of the tub and started toweling him off, he saw it as a golden opportunity for a little last-minute rough-house before his dad went away. He yelled, "Surprise attack!" and gave my stomach a friendly head butt. My stomach actually took it well, but Lev slipped on the wet floor and began to fall backward, his head threatening to land on the rim of our old bathtub. Moving instinctively, I managed to place my hand on the rim of the tub in time to cushion the blow.

Lev came out of that violent adventure unscathed, and so did I, except for a small cut on the back of my left hand. Since our ancient bathtub had some brown rust spots on the rim, I had to go to a nearby clinic for a tetanus shot. I managed to get it done quickly so I could make it back home for Lev's bedtime. Lev, already lying in bed in his pajamas, was upset. "They gave you an injection?" he asked. I nodded.

"And it hurt?"

"A little," I said.

"It's not fair," Lev shouted. "It's just not fair! I was the one carrying on. I should've gotten the scratch and the injection, not you. Why did you even put your hand there?"

I told Lev that I did it to protect him. "I know that," he said, "but why, why did you want to protect me?"

"Because I love you," I said, "because you're my son. Because a father always has to protect his son."

"But why?" Lev persisted. "Why does a father have to protect his son?"

I thought for a moment before answering. "Look," I said as

I stroked his cheek, "the world we live in can sometimes be very tough. And it's only fair that everyone who's born into it should have at least one person who'll be there to protect him."

"What about you?" Lev asked. "Who'll protect you now that Grandpa's dead?" I didn't cry in front of Lev. But later that night, on the plane to Los Angeles, I did. The guy at the airline counter at Ben Gurion Airport had suggested that I take my small suitcase onto the plane, but I didn't feel like schlepping it with me, so I checked it. After we landed and I waited in vain at the luggage carousel, I realized that I should have listened to him. There wasn't much in the suitcase: underwear, socks, a few ironed, neatly folded shirts for my readings, and a pair of my father's shoes. The truth is that my original plan was to bring a picture of him with me on the tour, but somehow, for no logical reason, a minute before I went downstairs to the cab, I shoved a pair of shoes that he'd left at my place a few months earlier into the suitcase instead. Now those shoes were probably circling around on some carousel in a different airport.

It took the airlines a week to return my suitcase, a week during which I'd participated in many events, given lots of interviews, and slept very little. My jet lag provided a great excuse, even though I must admit that even in Israel, before I left, I hadn't been sleeping very well. I decided to celebrate the emotional reunion between me and my luggage in New York with a long, hot shower. I opened my suitcase and the first thing I saw were my father's shoes, lying on a pile of ironed shirts. I took them out and put them on the desk. I picked out an undershirt and a pair of briefs and went into the bathroom. I came out ten minutes later to a flood: The entire floor of my room was covered with water.

A rare problem with the pipes, the mustached hotel maintenance guy would tell me later in a heavy Polish accent. Everything that was in my suitcase, which I'd left on the floor, was soaking wet. It was a good thing I'd tossed my jeans on the bed and hung my underwear on the towel rack.

The car that was coming to take me to the event was due in a few minutes, just enough time to dry a pair of socks with the hairdryer and discover how useless that was because my shoes were sitting on the bottom of the murky pool my room had become. The driver called me on my cell phone. He'd just arrived and had no good place to wait, so he wanted to know how long it would take me to come down. I glanced at my father's shoes resting on the desk, dry; they looked very comfortable. I put them on and tied the laces. They fit perfectly.

# Jam

The waitress in the Warsaw café asks if I'm a tourist. "The truth is," I tell her, pointing to the nearby intersection, "my home is right there." It's surprising how little time it's taken me to call the forty-seven-inch-wide space in a foreign country whose language I don't speak "home." But that long, narrow space where I spent the night really does feel like home.

Only three years ago, the idea sounded more like a silly prank. I got a call on my cell phone from a blocked number. On the other end of the line, a man speaking English with a thick Polish accent introduced himself as Jakub Szczęsny, and said that he was a Polish architect.

"One day," he said, "I was walking on Chłodna Street and saw a narrow gap between two buildings. And that gap told me that I had to build you a house there."

"Great," I said, trying to sound serious, "it's always a good idea to do what the gap tells you."

Two weeks after that weird conversation, which I filed away in my memory under "Unclear Practical Jokes," I received another call from Szczęsny. This time, it turned out, he was calling from Tel Aviv. He'd come here so that we could meet face-to-face because he thought, correctly, that I hadn't taken him seriously enough during our last conversation. When we met in a café on Ben Yehuda Street, he gave me more details about his idea of building a house for me that would have the proportions of my stories: as minimalist and small as possible. When Szczęsny saw the unused space between the two buildings on Chłodna Street, he decided that he had to build a home for me there. When we met, he showed me the building plans: a narrow, three-story house.

After our meeting, I took the computer-simulated picture of the house in Warsaw to my parents' house. My mother was born in Warsaw in 1934. When the war broke out, she and her family ended up in the ghetto. As a child, she had to find ways to support her parents and baby brother. Children could escape from the ghetto more easily and then smuggle food back in. During the war, she lost her mother and little brother. Then she lost her father, too, and was left completely alone in the world.

She once told me, many years ago, that after her mother had died, she told her father that she didn't want to fight anymore, that she didn't care if she died, too. Her father told her that she must not die, that she had to survive. "The Nazis," he said, "want to erase our family name from the land, and you're the only one who can keep it alive. It is your mission to get through the war and make sure that our name survives. So that everyone who walks down the streets of Warsaw knows it." Not long after that, he died in the Polish uprising. When the war ended, my mother was sent to an orphanage in Poland, then to one in France, and from there to Israel. By surviving, she fulfilled her father's request.

She kept the family and their name alive.

When my books began to appear in translation, the two countries in which, somewhat surprisingly, I became more successful as a writer were Poland and Germany. Later, conforming perfectly to my mother's biography, they were joined by France. My mother never went back to Poland, but my success in her native land was very important to her, even more important than my success in Israel. I remember that, after reading my first collection in Polish translation, she said to me, "You're not an Israeli writer at all. You're a Polish writer in exile."

My mother looked at the picture for less than a fraction of a second. To my surprise, she recognized the street immediately: the narrow home would be built, totally by chance, on the spot where a bridge had linked the small ghetto to the larger one. When my mother smuggled in food for her parents, she had to get past a barricade there, manned by Nazi soldiers. She knew that if she was caught carrying a loaf of bread, they'd kill her on the spot.

And now I'm here, at the same intersection, and that narrow house is no longer a simulation. Near the bell there's a sign that says, in big, brash letters, DOM KERETE (THE KERET HOUSE).

And I feel that my mother and I have now fulfilled my grandfather's wish, and our name is alive again in the city where almost no trace of my family is left.

When I come back from the café, waiting for me at the entrance is a neighbor, a woman even older than my mother, holding a jar. She lives across the street, heard about the narrow house, and wanted to welcome the new Israeli neighbor with some jam she made herself. I thank her and explain that my stay in the house will be limited and symbolic. She nods but isn't really listening to me. The guy I asked on the street to translate her Polish into English stops translating my words, and says in an apologetic tone that he thinks she doesn't really hear too well. I thank the woman again and turn to go into the house. She grabs my hand and launches into a long monologue. The guy translating into English can hardly keep up with her. "She says," the guy tells me, "that when she was a girl, she had two classmates who lived not far from here. Both girls were Jewish, and when the Germans invaded the city, they had to move to the ghetto. Before they left, her mother made them two jam sandwiches and asked her to give them to her girlfriends. They took the sandwiches and thanked her, and she never saw them again."

The old woman nods, as if confirming everything he's saying in English, and when he finishes, she adds another few sentences, which he translates. "She says that the jam she gave you is exactly the same kind her mother put in the girls' sandwiches. But times have changed, and she hopes they'll never force you to leave here." The old woman keeps nodding, and her eyes fill with tears. The hug I give her scares her at first, but then makes her happy.

That night I sit in the kitchen of my narrow house drinking a cup of tea and eating a slice of bread and jam that is sweet with generosity and sour with memories. I'm still eating when my cell phone vibrates on the table. I look at the display—it's my mother. "Where are you?" she asks in that worried tone she used to have when I was a kid and was late getting home from a friend's house.

"I'm here, Mom," I reply in a choked voice, "in our home in Warsaw."

# Fare and Good

**M**y wife says that I'm too nice, while I claim that she's just a very, very bad person. Around the time we started living together, we had a serious fight about it. It started when I came upstairs with a cabdriver who'd taken me home from the university. He had to pee. She awoke to the sound of his flushing the toilet, and she walked into our living room not fully dressed. The skinny cabdriver came out of the bathroom and gave her a polite "Good morning" while zipping up. She responded with a quick "Oh my God" and ran back into the bedroom.

The argument started after Skinny left. She said it was crazy to bring a cabbie you barely know into the house to use the bathroom. I said it was mean not to. After all, the entire field of taxi transportation is based on consideration of the passengers' feelings. Those cabbies drive around the streets all day without toilets on board, so where did she expect them to relieve themselves, in the trunk? As long as we focused on her claim that I was crazy, the discussion was quite civilized. But the minute I brought up the opposing hypothesis—that maybe most of humanity invites cabdrivers to use their bathroom, and only the selfish people among us, like her, for example, think it's weird—the decibel level began to rise.

It ended with our making a list of six mutual friends whom we would ask the same question: Have you ever invited a cabdriver up to your apartment to use your bathroom? If the majority said yes, I could keep inviting cabbies into our home. If the majority said no, I'd stop. And in case of a tie, I could keep on inviting them up, but I'd have to apologize to my wife for saying she's a bad person and give her a foot massage every day for a week.

We asked our six friends. They were all on her side. But what do you do if you're in a cab with a driver who really, really needs to go to the bathroom? I asked each of them. You just look the other way? You pay him and say, "Keep the change, man, and keep driving till you find yourself sitting in the middle of a little puddle"? Only then did I realize that I was endowed with the unique and absolutely insignificant power to sense when people need to go to the bathroom. It turned out that to me things like that were as transparent as those glass doors at the bank my wife keeps crashing into, while the rest of the human race is totally insensitive to the status of other people's bladders.

This happened eleven years ago, but last Friday, driving to Amnon's wedding at Kibbutz Shefayim, I remembered it. Amnon and I worked out at the same gym for almost two weeks before I quit. The only reason I know his name is Amnon is that the first time I met him, the gym owner said to him, "Hey, Amnon, how about trying a little deodorant?" And after a second's pause, he added, "Tell me, Etgar, that smell, isn't it criminal?" I told the gym owner that I didn't smell anything, and ever since, Amnon and I have been sort of friends. The truth is that when he gave me an invitation the last time I bumped into him in the neighborhood café, I was a little surprised. But it's like a subpoena—the minute the envelope touches your hand, you know you have to show up. That's the thing about wedding invitations—the less you know the person inviting you, the more obligated you feel to go. If you don't show up at your brother's wedding and say, "I couldn't come because the kid had chest pains and I took him to the ER," he'll believe you because he knows there's nothing you want more than to be there with him on his big day, but if it's an Amnon you hardly know, he'll realize right away that it's an excuse.

"I'm not going to the wedding of some smelly guy from your gym," my wife said, her tone determined.

"OK," I said, "I'll go alone. But next time we argue and I tell you that—"

"Don't say I'm a bad person again," she warned me. "I hate it when you do that." So, I don't say it, but I think it, all the way to the wedding at Kibbutz Shefayim. I won't be able to stay for very long. The invitation said the chuppah would be at twelve, and at one p.m. there's going to be a screening of my former student's film at the Cinematheque in Tel Aviv.

With the usually light Friday noon traffic, Shefayim to Tel Aviv takes half an hour, tops, so I'm sure I'll be covered. Except that it's already twelve-thirty, and the chuppah is showing no signs of starting. The student who directed the film has called three times to ask when I'll be there. More accurately, he called twice, and his older brother, whom I don't even know, called the third time to thank me for agreeing to come. "He didn't invite any of his other teachers to this screening," he told me, "just family, friends, and you." I decide to cut out. After all, Amnon saw me here, and I've already given a check.

As I get into the cab, I text my student that I might be a few minutes late. He texts me back that it's OK. They have some technical problems, and the screening will be delayed at least an hour. I ask the cabdriver to make a U-turn and go back to the wedding hall. The chuppah has just ended. I go over to Amnon and his bride and congratulate them. He hugs me, looking really happy. I know it wasn't nice of my wife to say he's "smelly"; he's a great person with feelings and all that, but the truth is that he does have a strong body odor.

Later, during the screening, I get a text message from my wife. "Where are you? The Druckers are waiting. Shabbat starts soon and they have to make it back to Jerusalem." The Druckers are friends who have become religious. Years ago, we used to smoke together. Today we mostly talk about kids. They have so many. And all of them, thank God, are healthy and sweet. I sidle toward the exit. My student saw me come in. That's enough. In an hour, I'll text him that it was great, and that I had to take off right after the screening. Sitting near the exit door is his brother. He looks at me as I leave. His eyes are wet with tears. He isn't crying because of me; he's crying because of the film. With all that pressure, I hardly noticed that they were screening one. If he's crying, it must be really good.

On the cab ride home, the driver talks constantly about the riots in Syria. He admits that he doesn't know who's against whom there, but he's excited about all the action. He talks and talks and talks, but the only thing I'm really listening to is his body. The guy's dying to pee. When we get to my house, the meter shows thirty-eight shekels. I give him a fifty-shekel note and tell him to keep the change. From the car window, I can see my wife on the balcony, laughing with Dror and Rakefet Drucker. She's not really a bad person.

# Pastrami

The air-raid siren catches us on the highway, driving to Shira's father's place north of Tel Aviv. Shira pulls over to the side of the road and we get out of the car, leaving the badminton rackets and feathered ball on the backseat. Lev holds my hand and says, "Daddy, I'm a little nervous." He's seven, and seven is the age when it's not considered cool to talk about fear, so the word *nervous* is used instead. Following Home Front Command instructions, Shira lies down on the side of the road. I tell Lev that he has to lie down, too. But he keeps standing there, his small, sweaty hand clutching mine. "Lie down already," Shira says, raising her voice to be heard over the blaring siren. He doesn't, and I remain standing, too.

"How'd you like to play a game of Pastrami Sandwich?" I ask Lev. "What's that?" he asks, not letting go of my hand.

"Mommy and I are slices of bread," I explain, "and you're a slice of pastrami, and we have to make a pastrami sandwich as fast as we can. Let's go. First, you lie down on Mommy," I say, and Lev lies down on Shira's back and hugs her as hard as he can. I lie on top of them, pressing against the damp earth with my hands so as not to crush them.

"This feels good," Lev says, and smiles.

"Being the pastrami is the best," Shira says under him.

"Pastrami!" I yell.

"Pastrami!" my wife yells.

"Pastrami!" Lev yells, his voice shaky, either from excitement or fear. "Daddy," Lev says, "look, there are ants crawling on Mommy."

"Pastrami with ants!" I yell.

"Pastrami with ants!" my wife yells.

*"Yech!"* Lev yells.

And then we hear the boom. Loud, but far away. We stay lying one on top of the other, without moving, for a long time. My arms are starting to hurt from carrying my weight. From the corner of my eye, I can see other drivers who've been lying on the highway get up and brush the dirt off their clothes. I start to stand up.

"Lie down," Lev tells me, "lie down, Daddy. You're ruining the sandwich."

I lie down for another minute, and say, "Okay, game's over. We won."

"But it's nice," Lev says. "Let's stay like this a little more."

We stay like that a few seconds longer. Mommy on the bottom, Daddy on the top, and Lev and a few red ants in the middle. When we finally get up, Lev asks where the rocket is.

I point in the direction from which the explosion came. "It sounded like it exploded not far from our house," I say.

"Oof," Lev says, disappointed, "now Lahav will probably find pieces again. Yesterday, he came to school with a piece of iron from the last rocket, and it had the symbol of the company on it and the name in Arabic. Why did it have to explode so far away?"

"Better far away than close by," Shira says as she wipes sand and ants off her pants.

"The best would be if it was far enough away so nothing happens to us, but close enough so I could pick up some pieces," Lev sums up.

"The best would be badminton on Grandpa Yonatan's lawn," I disagree with him, and open the door to the backseat of the car.

"Daddy," Lev says as I'm buckling him in, "promise that if there's another siren, you and Mommy will play Pastrami with me again."

"I promise," I say, "and if it gets boring, I'll teach you how to play Grilled Cheese."

"Great!" Lev says, and a second later, he adds more seriously, "but what if there aren't any more sirens ever?"

"I think there'll be at least one or two more. Don't worry," I reassure him. "And if not," Shira adds from the front seat, "we can play it without the sirens, too."

## ABOUT THE AUTHOR

Etgar Keret was born in Ramat Gan and now lives in Tel Aviv. A winner of the French Chevalier des Arts et des Lettres, he is a lecturer at Ben-Gurion University of the Negev and the author, most recently, of the story collection *Suddenly, a Knock on the Door*. His work has been translated into thirty-seven languages and has appeared in *The New Yorker*, *The Wall Street Journal*, *The Paris Review*, and *The New York Times*, among many other publications, and on *This American Life*, where he is a regular contributor.